CULTS AND NONCONVENTIONAL RELIGIOUS GROUPS

A COLLECTION OF OUTSTANDING STUDIES

edited by

J. GORDON MELTON
INSTITUTE FOR THE STUDY
OF AMERICAN RELIGION

A GARLAND SERIES

THE CHURCH OF GOD AND SAINTS OF CHRIST

THE RISE OF BLACK JEWS

———————————

ELLY M. WYNIA

GARLAND PUBLISHING, INC.
NEW YORK & LONDON / 1994

Library of Congress Cataloging-in-Publication Data

Wynia, Elly M., 1963–
    The Church of God and Saints of Christ : the rise of Black Jews /
Elly M. Wynia
       p.   cm. — (Cults and nonconventional religious groups)
    Includes bibliographical references.
    ISBN 0–8153–1136–2
    1. Church of God and Saints of Christ.   2. Crowdy, William
Saunders, 1847–1908.   3. Cults—United States.   4. Afro-American
Jews—History—20th century.   5. Afro-Americans—Religion.
6. Jewish Christians—United States—History—20th century.
I. Title. II. Title: Black Jews. III. Series.
BX7052.W96   1994
289.9—dc20   94–486
                                             CIP

Printed on acid-free, 250-year-life paper
Manufactured in the United States of America

Contents

Chapter

Preface

This project could not have been completed without the help of many individuals. Most essential was the help and guidance of Professor Timothy Miller. His encouragement was imperative for the completion of this project. Professor Miller's expertise in the area of New Religious Movements allowed for an excellent learning process of critical thinking and evaluation within the realms of religious history.

Special thanks to the many librarians of The Topeka State Historical Society, The Watson Library and The Spencer Library (Kansas Collection), both at the University of Kansas. All of the librarians were extremely helpful and willing to aid me in this endeavour. The Watkins Community Museum provided much information about Lawrence through various documents and the assistance of Steve Jansen.

The National Endowment for the Humanities Younger Scholars Award provided a grant which enabled me to visit the tabernacle and headquarters in Suffolk/Portsmouth, Virginia. The University of Kansas Research Awards for the Spring and Summer of 1988 were responsible for a tabernacle visit to Providence, Rhode Island. These three awards also provided the ability to drive to and from Topeka, pay for various long distance phone calls, and helped with the expense of photocopies.

I am indebted to Elder Preston Mangana and Rabbi John Eaves. Their cooperation in assisting me with the history of their church was invaluable.

George and Rebekah have sacrificed for over a year in seeing this project through to completion. Thank you.

Introduction

The Church of God and Saints of Christ was founded in Lawrence, Kansas on November 5, 1896 by William Saunders Crowdy. Crowdy was born at Charlotte Hall, St. Mary's County, Maryland in 1847, the son of slaves. During the first forty-five years of his life, Crowdy was a Baptist. In 1892, however, he began to have visions about establishing the "true church." Soon thereafter, he headed east to live in Kansas City with his wife's family while working as a hotel cook for the Santa Fe Railroad. During this time he began preaching in the surrounding area about this new church. Lawrence, Kansas was one of the places that Crowdy preached and it was there that the first tabernacle was established. His fervor allowed him to establish many churches and before his death in 1908 (at age 61) he had effectively routinized his charisma.

Since its initial formation in Kansas, the Church of God and Saints of Christ has spread widely in the United States and abroad. In the U.S. there have been at least 213 individual churches and as many as 37,000 members. Currently the majority of the churches are located on the East Coast. The church has its headquarters in Belleville (within the city of Portsmouth), Virginia. Outside the United States the church exists in the West Indies and in South Africa. Both of these regions have conditions that facilitate the expansion of this unique religious movement.

The most unusual feature of the faith of the Church of God and Saints of Christ is its synthesis of Jewish and Christian elements. The Jewish element is of particular interest in that the church is apparently the earliest example of so-called black Judaism in America. Crowdy taught that a variety of Jewish traditions must be preserved including celebrating the Sabbath on Saturday, adhering to all 613 laws of the Torah and observation of all Jewish holidays.

A careful scholarly study of this group is important for a number of reasons. First, there has been little serious research done on the Church of God and Saints of Christ. What little work has been done is either very specific (dealing with one particular element of the movement such as its music) or not well supported with reliable data. This work presents basic information and documentation on the COGSOC as a basis for ongoing research on the group.

Second, the combination of Judaism and Christianity that provides the theological foundation of this movement is distinctive, even unique. An analysis of the group's eclectic theology, understood in terms of the surrounding historical circumstances, will help clarify and illumine the role of religion in slave emancipation and black liberation.

Third, specific motifs can be identified in this group's sociological and theological development that demonstrate that one of its central themes was and is black emancipation. Yet nowhere in the historical accounts of either slave emancipation or the various elements of the civil rights movements has this church been so much as mentioned. Thus, establishing a general history of this group, one that involves a theological and sociological analysis, will fill an important gap in American black history.

Much of this book is based on the primary sources I have found at the Kansas State Historical Society. These sources were donated by Beersheba Granison, the granddaughter of Crowdy. The sources include minutes of church meetings, a sketchy biography of Crowdy's life, directories, funeral bulletins, manuals, newsletters, song books and temple dedication programs. In addition to this material I have located further primary sources, both written and oral, through contact with members of the organization. From these sources I have composed a general history of the church. I will amplify this general account by supplying information from church members and others with whom I have established contact. The sparseness, both in quantity and quality, of secondary sources testifies to the lack of scholarly research that has been done to date on the church. This book, then, will help fill that historical gap and provide basic information which should be useful to later scholars.

The Church of God
and Saints of Christ

Black Conditions from the
Civil War to 1900

> Under the pressure of federal bayonets, urged on
> by the misdirected sympathies of the world in
> behalf of the enslaved African, the people of
> Mississippi have abolished the institution of
> slavery . . . We must now meet the question as
> it is, and not as we would like to have
> it . . . The negro is free, whether we like it or
> not . . . To be free, however, does not make
> him a citizen, or entitle him to social or political
> equality with the white man.
> — The Black Code of Mississippi[1]

This excerpt from The Black Code of Mississippi
characterizes the stark conditions faced by the "freed" slaves.
The Emancipation Proclamation mandated the release of
southern slaves. However, there is a substantial gap between
release from bondage and achieving real freedom.[2] The
difference between formal and substantive freedom is
nowhere more evident than in the post-civil war black
situation. In this section I will discuss briefly some of the
main features of that situation. My focus will be the
condition of southern blacks, the population most pertinent
to this essay. My purpose is to outline the conditions faced
by the predecessors of William Saunders Crowdy and by
Crowdy himself. Thus it becomes possible to see why a
religious solution to these conditions was in many ways
more appealing than a political one was.

Although the Civil War ended in 1865, the United States continued to suffer its consequences for some time thereafter. As a nation, the U.S. was ideologically fragmented[3] and spiritually broken; its resources and infrastructure were riddled by war. The South in particular was in a state of disarray. It suffered far more physical damage than the North. And losing the war meant that the people of the south also lost much of their social and cultural identity. Most significantly, perhaps, the southern economy was irreversibly wounded; operating a plantation turned out to be very difficult without slave labor.

Abraham Lincoln, confident of victory and aware of the problems that would arise at the end of the war, issued his first reconstruction proposal, "Proclamation of Amnesty and Reconstruction" (The Ten Percent Plan) more than a year before the war ended. Its objective was to reunify the United States as rapidly as possible. The plan made it relatively easy for southern states to reenter the Union and for southern individuals to become full participants in the political process.[4] It is important to note that in the early phases of Reconstruction the emphasis was placed on national integrity, not racial equality. No initial provision that would encourage the integration of blacks into the American political process and American society was successfully incorporated into Reconstruction.[5]

The passage of the 13th amendment in 1865 effectively prohibited slavery. Thus southern blacks had a new-found freedom. However, it did not provide genuine liberation. A constitutional amendment without appropriate administrative procedures is little more than a legal abstraction. Lincoln, and his successor Andrew Johnson, knew that pressing for the full set of human rights for blacks would enrage southerners and slow the process of reconstruction. Hence allowances were made which ensured that the former slaves would be tightly controlled by the racist legal and political structures and social attitudes that prevailed in the South.

Prior to the adoption of the 13th amendment the prospect of freedom sparked hope in the slave population. The slaves wanted desperately to gain control of their own destinies.

The following passage from a letter written by General Nathaniel P. Banks to James McKaye exemplifies the enthusiasm of the potential freedmen and their supporters:

> I entertain no doubt whatever of the capabilities of the emancipated colored people to meet and discharge the duties incident to the great change in their condition. I have seen them in all situations, within the last year and a half, and it is with much pleasure I say as I stated to you in person, that they seem to me to have a clearer comprehension of their position, and the duties which rest upon them, than any other class of our people, accepting the necessity of labor which rests upon them as upon others. The conditions they uniformly impose show the good sense with which they approach the change in their condition.[6]

The emphasis was always placed upon the slave's capacity to earn a livelihood as a free individual. The ability to earn a living was both the dream of the slave and the argumentative platform of those promoting their emancipation. In order for it to happen, however, careful attention needed to be paid to actual conditions in the south. That became the political agenda of the radical Republicans in the late 1860's and early 1870's.[7]

Initially the efforts of the radical Republicans were thwarted by executive power. Andrew Johnson's reconstruction plan had conditions similar to Lincoln's (minimal at best) but he lacked the political finesse necessary to see that they were met. As a result, white southerners took advantage of the federal government's inability to enforce even these minimal constraints and blacks suffered. Large numbers of blacks were forced for one reason or another to live in crowded shantytowns under oppressive conditions.[8] Congressional awareness of these conditions prompted the establishment of the Freedmen's Bureau in March, 1865.

The objective of the Bureau, and the accompanying legislative act, was to moderate the shift from slavery to freedom. Included in the establishing act were a number of provisions that proposed to facilitate redistribution of wealth in the south.[9] But such provisions were not well received by southern whites. Hence they presented a threat to the reconstruction process (and the dominant theme of national integrity) and became expendable. Given the lack of a firm national policy with respect to the freedmen, the people of the south were, as Gruver put it, able "to keep the ex-slaves in a position of economic, social and political inferiority."[10] The legal measures taken to ensure this were called the "Black Codes." Their primary objective was to maintain blacks as social and political subordinates.

Great efforts were made, at the political level,[11] by the radical Republicans to alter the established course of reconstruction. Some of the victories that they laid claim to included the passage of the 14th and 15th amendments to the constitution. These certainly improved the political status of blacks — allowing them to participate more freely in processes that were to determine their fate. This was particularly the case at the state level where politically active blacks made substantial contributions to the ongoing process of reconstruction. But the initial ambivalence (on the part of the federal government) with respect to issues pertaining to racial equality and the ongoing united front of stalwart white southerners against equality soon began to take its toll. A sophisticated network of secret societies, the most prominent of which was the Ku Klux Klan, began developing immediately after the war and was able to effectively keep blacks in subordinate positions. Through threatened and actual violence they controlled the political process.[12] The following excerpt from the testimony of a black politician, Alexander K. Davis, before a congressional subcommittee investigating the Klan illustrates the tactics that were utilized.

> The character of them was about this: I will not say that I know of them — threats being made of that kind, but I have heard of threats being made

> that this Klan would see to the negroes voting, or
> how they voted.I have had gentlemen to tell me,
> right on the streets here, that we would not be
> able to carry this county; though we had a
> majority of two thousand in the county, that we
> would never be able to carry it again.[13]

Illegal clandestine activity prevented black southerners from achieving the gains that they might have had the political climate been less infected. Later, as the black vote became less useful due to changes in the economic and political conditions in the south, many of the legal formalities, which could have made substantial contributions to the black condition if the political climate at the local level had not been so corrupt, were deferred through local laws which were upheld by the Supreme Court.[14] The broader message that this sent to blacks is that freedom is difficult to achieve through the political channels that are the product of racist white individuals. As a result, liberation was often sought through a higher source.[15]

The religious formation of the post-civil war blacks took place during the period of slavery. Depending on the convictions of the master, slaves were often exposed to a highly edited version of Christianity which was used to convince them that their situation was the will of God.[16] This was not the full extent of their religious experience, however. In their own worship services the slaves emphasized themes that had liberation and a strong sense of community at their core. As John Blassingame put it

> Most slaves, repelled by the brand of religion
> their masters taught, formulated new ideas and
> practices in the quarters. The slave's religious
> principles were colored by his own longings for
> freedom and based on half-understood sermons
> in white churches or passages from the Old
> Testament, struggles of the Jews, beautiful
> pictures of a future life, enchantment and fear,

and condemnation of sin. Frequently the praise
meetings started on Saturday or Sunday evenings
and lasted far into the nights.[17]

Religious practices of the sort here described carried over
into the post-slavery period. It was the hope secured by their
faith that helped the blacks continue their quest for freedom
in the face of dismal political obstacles.[18]

A great deal of emphasis during the post-reconstruction
period was placed on salvation in the afterlife and ecstatic
experience in this life. The services themselves had a
cathartic effect on the participants. Internal tension, built up
in one's soul under conditions of repression, could be
expunged in the worship service. As one observer wrote,

> The shouting now became general; a dozen or
> more entering into it most heartily. These
> demonstrations increased or abated, according to
> movements of the leaders, who were in and
> about the pulpit; for the minister had closed his
> discourse, and first one, and then another would
> engage in prayer. The meeting was kept up till a
> late hour, during which, four or five sisters
> becoming exhausted, had fallen upon the floor
> and lay there, or had been removed by their
> friends.[19]

But these themes did not constitute the entire content of
the post-reconstruction black religious experience. There
was a deep understanding of their own state of oppression
among the blacks which prompted a sense of identity with
the oppressed children of Israel. The Old Testament themes
that had carried them through the period of slavery with the
hope of a "promised land" continued to inform their religious
consciousness. And it was this consciousness which
provided the receptacle for the prophetic teachings of W.S.
Crowdy.[20] Before I discuss those teachings, however, I will
briefly outline some of the basic tenets of Judaism and show

why they were pertinent to the black situation in the post-reconstruction south.

Notes

[1] Lincoln had no grand aspirations to free the slaves;the purpose of fighting the war was to preserve the integrity of the union. In fact, originally he planned to create a colony outside of the United States for the slaves. Lincoln, however, needed to carefully administer the various factions that comprised his base of support. The preliminary emancipation proclamation masterfully achieved this. While it did little to actually change conditions in the south it did pacify the radical abolitionist, drew support from anti-slavery groups in England and prompted a large number of blacks in the free states to volunteer their services to the Union's military forces. From these facts it can easily be inferred that the objectives of the document had little or nothing to do with "emancipation." See Rebecca Brooks Gruver's *An American History* (Reading: Addison-Wesley Pub. Co., 1978), 282–284.

[2] It is interesting to note in this context that the Exodus narrative which is so fundamental to any Jewish-based theology deals extensively with this gap. Being delivered "out of the house of bondage" and actually finding "the promised land" are two significantly different phenomena. I will discuss the Exodus theme more extensively in the next section.

[3] I use the phrase "ideologically fragmented" in reference to a variety of splits and factions. There is of course the obvious split between northerners and southerners with respect to the issue of abolition. But, there were also factions within the Republican party--the moderates and the abolitionists — and a gap between the executive and legislative branch of the government that created problems that were manifest during the reconstruction process. For an account of the various factions and the problems created by infighting see Gruver, pp 289–292 and Leslie H. Fishel jr. and Benjamin Quartes *The Black American* (New York: William Morrow, 1970), 258–263.

[4] Lincoln's plan prevented only high confederate officials from participating in the political process. "All high civilian and military officials would be permanently barred from participating in the political process" (Gruver, p. 290). Quite a battle developed between the president and Congress on this issue. Lincoln's plan required that only ten percent of the citizens of a state that had previously voted swear allegiance to the Union prior to being readmitted. Congress, however passed a much harsher bill (Wade-Davis) that required fifty percent of previously voting citizens to swear allegiance and significantly limited the degree of political participation allowed. Lincoln countered this move by letting the bill die by a pocket veto — increasing the tension between the executive and legislative branches (Gruver, pp. 290–291)

[5] The battle raged on among the radicals, the moderates and the conservative southerners. Eventually constitutional amendments, such as the 14th and 15th, were passed, as were further reconstruction plans forwarded by the radical Republicans (in 1867 and 1868). But it is important to note that these were not part of the original plan which staged the attitudes and practices of reintegrated southern states. The substance of the latter referendum is questionable as a result of this.

[6] Fishel and Quarles, p. 242.

[7] See Gruver, pp. 292–295.

[8] In 1865 as many as 100,000 blacks died of starvation and disease in shantytowns. See Gruver, page 292.

[9] One of the key elements of this proposal was "20 acres and a mule." This would provide a black family with the resources necessary for beginning an agricultural career. Unfortunately, an idea with such radical "socialist" underpinnings went contrary to the deeply ingrained notion of the sanctity of private property. Hence, it became a victim of reconstructive politics. See Gruver, page 292.

[10] Gruver, page 292.

[11] I add this clause to qualify the motivational force of the radical republicans. Certainly, they were somewhat concerned with the conditions faced by the freedmen. But they also were interested in establishing themselves as a political force. Often blacks were merely used as political pawns.

[12] This provides an interesting commentary on the nature of democracy in America. The question that I would raise in this context is: 'To what extent does this sort of plundering of the democratic process still take place and to what degree is it racially motivated?'. It is

virtually impossible to arrive at an accurate answer to this question it is worth noting that the presidential candidacy of Jesse Jackson in 1988 was labeled by the media and political analysts as impossible, insofar as the American people would never elect a black president regardless of his or her credentials.

[13] Fishel and Quarels, page 281.

[14] The economic and political conditions that I am referring to are respectively the agricultural depression of the late 80's and early 90's and the respondent rise, and battle against, "populism." The local legislation of specific importance includes poll taxes, literacy requirements for voting and rigid residency requirements. All of these were used to render blacks politically impotent. See Gruver, page 301.

[15] The data for this paragraph are abstracted from Fishel and Quarles, pp. 257–263, and Gruver, pp. 290–298 and 301–302.

[16] "White ministers taught the slaves that they did not deserve freedom, that it was God's will that they were enslaved, that the devil was creating these desires for liberty in their breasts, and that runaways would be expelled from the church. Then followed the slave beatitudes: blessed are the patient, blessed are the faithful, blessed are the cheerful, blessed are the submissive, blessed are the hardworking, and above all, blessed are the obedient." From John W. Blassingame, *The Slave Community* (New York: Oxford Press, 1972), 62–63.

[17] Blassingame, p. 64.

[18] It is interesting to note in this context that the slaves often perceived Lincoln to be a messianic figure. "Recently at Beaufort a gang of colored men, in the service of the quartermaster, at work on the wharf, were discussing the qualifications of the President, his wonderful power, how he had dispersed their masters, and what he would undoubtedly do hereafter for the colored race, when an aged, white headed negro, a "praise man" (as the phrase is) amongst them, with all the solemnity and earnestness of an old prophet, broke forth: 'What do you know bout Massa Linkum? Massa Linkum be ebrewhere. He walk de earth like de lord.'" (Fishel and Quarles, p. 249.) This is indicative of the way that black communities have historically blurred the distinction between spiritual and temporal emancipation, as well as that between religious and political activism. This lack of distinction has driven black communities to some of their greatest achievements right on through the civil rights movement of the 50's and 60's.

[19] Edited by Milton C. Sernett *Afro-American Religious History: A Documentary Witness* (Durham: Duke University Press, 1985), 240.

[20] Jesse E. Brown Jr. *Doctrinal Synopsis of the COGSOC* (Rochester: Colgate Rochester Divinity School, 1981), 2.

Black Judaism

By the year 1863, after almost 250 years of captive slavery, and by the year 1900, an additional 37 years of immoral slavery, the black people in this country were at a very low ebb. The words of the prophecy of Ezekiel fittingly described our dilemma in this way: "There were very many bones in the open valley, and lo, they were very spiritually and morally dry. For our bones are dried; and our hope is lost; and we are cut off from our parts." (Ezekiel 37:2&11)[1]

The Jewish components of American Christianity were appealing to slaves and to post-abolition blacks. They identified with the stories of the embondaged children of Israel and had hopes of God's leading them out of their state of slavery in a similar manner. In this section I will provide a more detailed account of the themes in Jewish theology that are appealing to blacks and point out some of the ways that they have been appropriated by black Jewish movements.

Several of the basic tenets of Judaism are pertinent to the conditions faced by blacks in America. Probably the most prominent is the Exodus theme. The precondition for an Exodus is a state of embondagement. In the traditional Jewish narrative the children of Israel were the slaves of the Egyptian Pharaoh. It was in this state that their collective identity was formed; they gained a sense of themselves as a "people." With this attitude established it was a united force that God led out of exile to an awaiting promised land.[2]

Another important element of Judaism is the unity and strength that Jewish people have experienced within their religiously founded community. The model is that of the extended family of which Abraham is the original patriarch. It is his ancestry which constitutes God's family on earth.[3]

> In historical terms Judaism is a family religion. For an orthodox family, the whole of life is dominated by the religious element.[4]

This tradition has been transferred from generation to generation down to the present. The following provides a testimonial to this effect from a contemporary Jew.

> There is in Judaism a relentless intensity about the importance of educating children, of passing on traditions, of bringing along the next generation to carry on whatever Jews define, in various ways, as the essence of their Jewish identity.[5]

Through this intense sense of community Jews have repeatedly survived situations that would have broken a less unified people.[6]

Finally, the Jewish conception of the Kingdom of God is important to this study. Speaking generally, the Kingdom of God is the period in which God reigns over humans. It is characterized by a state of peace and fellowship.[7] It is important to note that this theological theme is predicated on a political metaphor which is to become a political reality. This distinguishes the Jewish understanding of the Kingdom of God from that later formulated in Christianity.

These themes played an important role in the formation of black religious thought and practice. Blacks readily identified with the experience of being enslaved by tyrannical masters. Moreover, the prospect of a genuine exodus directed by God inspired leaders provided hope of liberation.

Similarly, blacks found great strength in the community networks that developed during the period of slavery. They achieved a sense of brotherhood and sisterhood which provided them with the courage to withstand hardship as well as the impetus to improve their condition. Like the children of Israel, the communal ties established during the period of embondagement provided the collective identity necessary to break free.

Finally, the belief that God would participate in struggles to improve their condition on earth is directly related to the Jewish hope that the Kingdom of God is to be realized in this world. This belief provided the hope necessary for persistent action in the face of adverse conditions.

While for the most part blacks in America have appropriated these important Jewish themes within some form of Christianity, there have been several examples of explicitly Jewish black religious movements. One example is Church of the Living God, founded by Prophet F. S. Cherry in 1915 in Philadelphia. He believed and taught that he and his followers were the descendants of the Old Testament patriarch Jacob (who Cherry claimed was black). His claim was that white people were merely masquerading as Jews. They were able to do this because the true Jews (the blacks) were not known to the world. He also taught that Christ was black.[8]

According to Israel J. Gerber, the best known black Jewish leader is Rabbi Wentworth A. Matthews, founder of The Commandment Keepers of the Royal Order of Ethiopian Hebrews. It was his belief that the Hebrews of the exodus were black. Also, he claimed that the ten tribes of Judah were dispersed throughout Africa. White Jews, he taught, are the descendants of Esau while black Jews fall from Jacob's lineage. This claim would require that Rebekah and Isaac produced twins of both black and white skin.[9]

According to Arthur Dobrin, the Moorish Zionist Temple of Brooklyn is the first example of black Judaism in America. It was founded by Rabbi Richlieu in 1899. While the previously mentioned groups (Cherry's and Matthew's) were exclusively black, Richlieu encouraged white participation as well. Dobrin's assertion that this is the first black Jewish group in America is based on the view that groups formed earlier than this that are called Jewish are in fact not. This is the case that he presents with respect to the Church of God and Saints of Christ.[10]

It is clear that Dobrin is mistaken in his assessment of the Church of God and Saints of Christ. Errors of fact undermine his case: he refers to the founder as William L. Crouder instead of William S. Crowdy; second, he claims that the church was founded in "Bellvue," Virginia, instead of Lawrence, Kansas; he characterizes Bishop Plummer as preaching anti-Semitic sermons; finally, he misidentifies Prophet Cherry as a central member of the Church of God and Saints of Christ. The description that he presents of Cherry's background is identical to that of Crowdy's.[11]

Another scholar, James E. Landing, claims that the Church of God and Saints of Christ is in fact the first black Jewish movement in the United States.[12] This assertion corresponds to my findings.[13] The claim of primacy belongs to Crowdy; the only question is whether or not the Church of God and Saints of Christ is actually a Jewish group. I will demonstrate in the following sections on the life of W. S. Crowdy and the theology of the church that in fact they have a distinctly Jewish dimension to them.

Notes

[1] Jesse E. Brown, "Doctrinal Synopsis of the COGSOC" (Rochester: Colgate Rochester Divinity School, 1981 — a term paper), p. 12.

[2] Leo Trepp, *Judaism: Development and Life* (Belmont: Wadsworth, 1982), p. 193.

[3] Lewis M. Hopfe, *Religions of the World* (Encino: Glenco Pub., 1979), p. 236.

[4] Hans-Joachin Schoeps, *The Religions of Mankind* (Garden City: Doubleday, 1968), p. 224.

[5] Frances D. Horowitz, "A Jewish Woman in Academic America," *Seeing Female: Social Roles and Personal Lives* (New York: Greenwood Press, 1986), p. 55.

[6] The most significant example of this is the way that the Jewish people were able to bounce back from the horrors of the holocaust.

[7] Trepp, p. 243.

[8] Israel Gerber, *The Heritage Seekers: Black Jews in Search of Identity* (Middle Village: Jonathon David Pub., 1977), p. 70. It is worth noting in this context that Cherry has been confused with Crowdy in Arthur Dobrin's *A History of Negro Jews in America* (Unpublished paper City College of the City University of New York 1965, Schamburg Collection, New York City Public Library).

[9] Gerber, p. 71.

[10] Dobrin, p. 31.

[11] Dobrin, p. 49.

[12] Landing made this claim in a letter (dated November 3, 1987) and will publish it in (Live Ever Die Never).

[13] This is verified in the following sources: *Black Jews in America*, "Christianity Today," 1973, "Black Jews: A House Divided" by James S. Tinney, Judaism, 1975, "Black Hebrew Israelites" by Robert Weisbord, *Encyclopedia of American Religions*, "Religion in Life" Vol. 28, Winter, 1958-1959, by Norman Eddy.

The Life of William Saunders Crowdy

It was during this period of turmoil, that Prophet Crowdy came and he said, "I just got down in time to save us (Israel) from an additional seventy years of bondage." Therefore, from 1893, when Prophet Crowdy received his very first vision from God, to 1963, the signing of the Civil Rights Bill, black people were enslaved in an Egypt of economic, political and civil oppression; enslaved in an Egypt of bigotry, hatred, insecurity and self-destruction. Their weakened bodies, their feeble knees and their chaffed necks were laboring under the yoke of the oppressors. Nevertheless, God still called as He did to Pharaoh, "Let my people go." Prophet Crowdy proceeded to equip us with a profound self-awareness and undergirded us with a dynamic God consciousness, hence, the re-establishment of the "Ancient of Days" in the minds of the lost sheep of the house of Israel.[1]

William Saunders Crowdy was born in Charlotte Hall, Saint Mary's County, Maryland in 1847 to Basle and Sarah Ann Crowdy. He grew up on the Chisly Hill Plants Farm, a slave plantation, where his mother was a cook.[2] His duties were those of a house boy. He escaped slavery in 1863 and headed northwest. He changed his name at this time from Wilson to William and joined the Union Army. His role was that of Quarter Master Corps officers' cook. After the Civil

War he purchased an 100 acre farm in Guthrie, Oklahoma and resumed his given name.[3]

Little information is available about Crowdy's education. One can surmise that he learned the rudiments of reading and writing; that was generally the extent of the education of young slaves. It is obvious that he had little sophisticated education. It is similarly obvious, however, that he was highly intelligent and a thinker of visionary proportions.

Crowdy's first religious experiences were most likely similar to those of other slaves at this time. It is unclear to what degree this influenced him but one can assume that the previously discussed Jewish themes that were so appealing to the slaves had an effect on him. In Guthrie he was a member of a Baptist church and served this congregation as a deacon. The connection between these experiences and his later visions is, however, not clear.

Around the mid 1890's Crowdy moved to Kansas City, Missouri, and began working as a cook at a hotel owned by the Sante Fe Railroad. At a church fair he met Lovey Yates Higgins whom shortly thereafter he married. They resided initially in the home of Lovey's mother where three children, Mattie Leah (who died young), Isaac, and August were born. Shortly after the birth of their third child the Crowdy family returned to Guthrie to resume an agricultural career.[4] Their farm income was supplemented by Crowdy's work as head cook in an English kitchen.[5]

In 1893, while still in Guthrie, Crowdy had begun to act in a peculiar manner. His wife suspected that he was drinking too much but in fact he was having the first waves of what later were interpreted as prophetic visions.

> He was actually physically frightened by the voices that talked to him and that told him what to do and about the things which would happen to him if he did not obey. It was many years before he learned that the voice was not of his imagination but actually the voice of God speaking to him.[6] Later the precise meaning of these experiences became clear to Crowdy.

Crowdy's first coherent vision took place in this same year on September 13th while he was clearing ground for a new crop.[7] He heard a loud sound that was similar to that produced by a large flock of birds. Amidst this noise he thought he heard a voice saying 'run for your life'. On hearing this he dropped his axe and cleared a trail into the forest with his mattock (because he thought that he was going to die and he wanted to be sure that his body would be found). There he fell into a deep slumber during which the vision came to him as a dream.

He dreamt that he was in a large room and that tables were descending from above. The tables were covered with filthy vomit (similar to Isaiah 28:8 where it says "For all tables are full of vomit and filthiness, so that there is no place clean."). Each table was labeled with the name of a church (e.g. Methodist, Baptist, etc.). The biggest and dirtiest table was labeled Baptist, prompting Crowdy to resolve never to attend a Baptist church again. At one point in the vision a small, clean white table came down with the name Church of God and Saints of Christ on it. Once it was firmly planted on solid ground it began to expand, displacing all the other tables. This was the sign to Crowdy that he was to establish a movement under this name which would be the "true" church. Later in the vision Crowdy received a set of rules and guidelines, now known as the Seven Keys, which he recorded on a tablet. The final significant element of the vision involved Crowdy's being presented with a Bible which he proceeded to eat. This signified, as in Revelation 10:2-10, that the entire Bible was written in him.[8] After the vision came to an end, Crowdy simply got up and returned to his home.[9]

Shortly after the visionary experience, Crowdy began preaching in the streets of Guthrie. He was amazed at his own knowledge and powers of communication. While the precise content of his preaching is not clear, it is safe to assume that he was beginning to communicate the vision that he had received with respect to establishing the "true" church. The course of action that he took began with the baptism of his family and was followed by the baptism of receptive citizens of Guthrie and individuals in the surrounding area.[10]

Between the years 1893 and 1896 Crowdy heard voices instructing him to leave Guthrie and spread the vision of his church. He ignored these voices, and he believed, as a result suffered a crop failure in 1895 which prompted him to heed their call. His wife thought that he was running off with another woman and therefore insisted that he take their eldest son Isaac with him. Together on horseback they headed for Texas as the "world's evangelists." While in Texas he preached everywhere he went. He was arrested twenty-three times (primarily because he was black); thus he extended his ministry into the prison system. According to Isaac Crowdy, while they were in one of these prisons, a light came and opened up the door of their cell. This signified to Crowdy that they were to leave Texas. Isaac was sent home to Guthrie while his father headed north to Chicago.[11]

While in Chicago, in 1896, Crowdy concentrated his ministerial efforts in the State Street region. There he spent a great deal of time actually preaching on the street. This resulted in the conversion of many people, a good portion of whom were white. During this time he came to be known as "the black Elijah." It was here that he received advice from a drunken Irishman telling him to organize so that the people that he baptized would have a structured religious organization within which they could practice their new faith. Crowdy chose to do so in Lawrence, Kansas.[12]

Crowdy arrived in Lawrence in the fall of 1896 (November 8th is the recognized establishment date for the church[13]). Lawrence, a city that was established in 1854,[14] provided a fruitful environment for Crowdy's ministry. This region received a large number of ex-slaves during the waves of emigration waves that followed the enactment of the 13th Amendment. Due to the fact that Kansas had been a free state it was perceived to be a friendly environment. In 1890 Lawrence had a population of 9994, 2155 of whom were black.[15] It is also clear that Lawrence had a well established network of religious organizations. The first of these formed was the Unitarian Church in 1854. Two black churches, Saint Luke AME and 9th Street Baptist, opened in 1862.[16] In short, the community provided a successful environment for establishing organized religions and there was a large body of black individuals for Crowdy to concentrate his ministerial efforts on.

Crowdy began preaching in Lawrence on the corner of 8th street and Massachusetts. He quickly made converts, and as more people were baptized the followers began to resemble an organized church. In 1897, at the Douglas County courthouse, a large meeting was held, which was arranged by John Lutz and a Mr. Jones.[17] At this meeting a large number of people were baptized. Crowdy preached from Luke 6:46: "Why call me lord, lord and do not the things I say?" It was here that he was inspired to spread his ministry throughout Kansas. He subsequently established churches in twenty-nine nearby cities.[18] On June 24th, 1898, the first annual general assembly was held in Emporia, Kansas. During this meeting, and a subsequent meeting in Lawrence on October 10, 1899, the church was formally organized.

Between 1896 and Crowdy's death in 1908 the church assumed the shape of a formal institution. It was during this period that Crowdy wrote the sermons that are now known as his epistles. The most notable of these is a sermon preached in Lawrence in 1903. Crowdy here urged the congregation to wage an unrelenting war against oppression and discrimination. The primary role of the "epistles" in the life of the church has been to provide guidance for behavior in specific types of situations. Some examples of this are "He Warns his Elders to Set Good Examples for the Members," "The Passover," "Get Your First Wives and Husbands," "One Man and One Woman Epistle," "Advice to the Sisters," "How to Leave and Fix Your House on the Sabbath," and "How Members are to Visit Other Tabernacles."[19]

Crowdy's reported prophesies and miracles have also provided a constitutive base for the organization.

Among his outstanding prophecies are the seven
warnings to the church in 1902, foretelling the
death of Queen Victoria, the great prophetic
sermon at Lawrence, Kansas, in 1903, the
assassination of President William McKinley and
the World War. He was also know for his
outstanding miracles, to wit: the raising of the
dead in Philadelphia, Pa., the calling back of the
water at Newark Bay, Newark, N.J., calling
down rain at Belleville, Va., in 1904, and at
Lawrence, Kansas, in 1903. He further stopped
the speech of John Christian, at the Washington,
D.C. Passover, in 1904, at the True Reformers'
Hall.[20]

Much of the content of Crowdy's prophecies has been
incorporated into the church's theology. The prophetic event
itself continues to inspire members of the tabernacles and
provides them with a deep sense of spirit. The organization
has and does place a great deal of emphasis on the figure of
Crowdy. His persona contributes significantly to the unity of
the group. Belief in the prophesies and miracles noted above
figure importantly in the preservation of Crowdy's influence
on the church.

Based on his vision, Crowdy believed that it was his
calling to formulate doctrinal standards for the "true church."
He claimed that black people were the true descendants of
the lost tribes of Israel. Also, he taught that through a literal
understanding of the Old and New Testaments, as well as
compliance with the Ten Commandments and the Seven
Keys, humanity could achieve salvation. Crowdy also
included in the church's doctrine an emphasis on observing
Jewish practices and holidays.[21]

Some of the tactics that Crowdy used in his street
preaching days carried over into the regular liturgy of the
church. One of the most prominent examples of this is the
prevalence of music. When preaching, Crowdy would often
break into song to attract the attention of people passing by.
Realizing that music had a powerful spiritual dimension, he

established it as a central element in the worship services of the church. Crowdy wrote some of the music that has been used by the group. His most famous song is "O Sinner Won't You Come."[22] This song deals with the problem of the poor and needy. Other important songs that bolster the church's liturgy include: "Prophet William Saunders Crowdy Said I Don't Want No Land," "The Farms We Have Got Em Back," and "It Was The Lord Speaking To the Prophet."[23] The interesting aspect of these songs is that they deal with the land in Belleville that the organization owns. They perceive this to be a "land of Canaan" which represents freedom and prosperity. It is significant that this theme is ingrained in the church's liturgy.

Crowdy wrote the church's formal constitution on October 10th, 1899 in Lawrence. The preamble of the constitution is also known as the Seven Keys. It reads as follows:

1. Repentance of sin.
2. Baptism by burial into water upon confession of faith.
3. Received unleavened bread and water for Christ's body and blood.
4. Feet washed by elder as is written in John 13:1–23.
5. Agree to keep commandments
6. Breathed upon with the holy kiss
7. Taught to pray as it is written in Matthew 6:9–13

This provides a behavioral prescription as well as a criterion for membership in the organization.

During Crowdy's life there were four General Assemblies held in Emporia and Lawrence, Kansas, and in Philadelphia. During these assemblies specific duties were determined for Bishops, Boards of Presbytery, Evangelists at Large, Evangelists, Ministers, and Members, and Laws were generated for governing tabernacles. He also established, at the first general assembly, *The Stone of Truth*, which (among other things) provided Jewish names for the months of the calendar. It was also at the Lawrence Assembly that the Episcopal form of hierarchical structure was established.

In 1900 Crowdy established the church's headquarters in Philadelphia, where he was joined by 5000 members. It was here that the first Passover was held at the Quaker City Hall in 1901.[24] Under his successor the headquarters was moved to Belleville, Virginia in 1917.

Crowdy died in Newark, New Jersey, on August 4th, 1908, at the residence of Chief Evangelist Malinda D. Morris (a former female Baptist preacher who had a large following in her tabernacle).[25] Crowdy was originally buried in Newark (at Rose St., near Bergen and 18th) but since then his grave has moved to Belleville, Virginia (across the street from Temple Beth El).[26] During the years prior to his death Crowdy had married a second wife, Saint Hallie Brooker,[27] with whom he had two children — William and Isabella. Crowdy renounced second marriages in a subsequent sermon, at which point he summoned his first wife to rejoin him and they spent the remainder of his life together. Some of Crowdy's other accomplishments in life include owning and operating a grocery store, a restaurant, a cafe, Noah's Ark Daughter's of Jerusalem furniture store, a printing office (where the Weekly Prophet was published), and a barbershop.[28] Crowdy used these ventures to contribute to the well being of his followers. They participated in various capacities in all of these businesses. This demonstrates the comprehensive concern that Crowdy had for the members of the church. In the spirit of the Jewish heritage which Crowdy appropriated, the distinction between spiritual and material well being was blurred.

Notes

[1] Jesse E. Brown, "Doctrinal Synopsis of The Church of God and Saints of Christ" (Rochester: Colgate Rochester Divinity School, 1981 — A term paper —), p. 13.

[2] No data is available on the role of Crowdy's father. It was common practice at this time to break up the families of slaves. My assumption is that this is what happened.

[3] Beersheba Crowdy Walker, *Life and Works of William Saunders Crowdy* (Philadelphia: Elfreth Walker, 1955), pp. 1–3.

[4] Walker, p. 3.

[5] *Business and Resident Directory of Guthrie and Logan County for the year Commencing Sept. 1, 1892* (Guthrie: Frankie G. Poutry Pub., 1892), p. 43.

[6] Walker, p. 4.

[7] *The Church of God and Saints of Christ Directory: 1896–1946* (In Honor of our 50th Anniversary — 1896–1946 —, Dedicated to Bishop H.Z. Plummer), p. 7.

[8] While it is not completely evident exactly how long the vision is supposed to have lasted, it was clearly at least several days.

[9] Walker, pp. 7–8.

[10] Ibid., p. 9.

[11] Ibid., p. 9–10.

[12] Ibid., p. 11.

[13] *Church of God and Saints of Christ Directory*, p. 43.

[14] Kaethe Schick and Kathy Hoggard, "The Black Community in Lawrence, 1870–1915" (an unpublished paper), p. 4.

[15] *12th Census of U.S. taken in 1900* (Washington: U.S. Census Office, 1901), p. 458.

[16] David Dary, *Lawrence Douglas County Kansas: An Informal History* p. 194. Dorothy Penington, *The Histories and Cultural Roles of Black Churches in Lawrence*, (Unpublished, 1983), p. 4. Steve Jansen (director of the Watkins Museum in downtown Lawrence), says

it is not clear which of the two black churches was first. There is some controversy over this issue.

[17] *Lawrence City Directory* (Sioux Center, Iowa: R.C. Polk Co., 1907–1913), pp. 13–18. John Lutz became pastor of the church in 1913 (1239 N.J.), before him Frank Smith was pastor (13E. Henry) until 1911 when J.M. Venarable was pastor. After Smith, Martin Fears was the last known Lawrence pastor from 1917 until 1919 (this being the last date that the church appears in the directories).

[18] Walker, p. 14. These cities were Emporia, Topeka, Strong City, Lawrence, Florence, Peabody, Newton, Wichita, Enterprise, Abilene, Salina, Ottawa, Chanute, Valley Falls, Osage City, Atchison, Leavenworth, Garden City, Wamego, Coffeyville, Arkansas City, Junction City, Larned, Manhattan, Dodge City, Girard and Lyons. In order to find out if there was any historical data about the church in any of these cities, I contacted the respective County Historical Societies. I have heard back from most of them with no new information.

[19] *Prophet William S. Crowdy's Great Prophetic Sermons — 1903*, pp. 12–19.

[20] Walker, p. 14.

[21] T.F. Murphy, *Census of Religious Bodies: 1936* (Washington D.C.: U.S. Government Printing Office, 1941), p. 439.

[22] *Prophet William Saunders Crowdy's Great Prophetic Sermons*, p. 21.

[23] *"I love thy church of God."* Songs taken by title from this collection of 126 pages of songs. See Appendix 4.17.

[24] Walker, p. 12.

[25] Walker, p. 34. Malinda was appointed chief Evangelist of the Daughters of Jerusalem by prophet Crowdy.

[26] "Black Jews step out of the shadows." *Virginian Pilot*, April 1, 1988.

[27] Walker, p. 39. Hallie Brooker was the assistant grand secretary of the church.

[28] Walker, p. 49.

The History of the Church

"Because He Came"

Evang C.C. Farrar — Nov. 5 1987

God sent a man, his name was Crowdy.
He came to bring back the ancient of days.
He said he just got down in time.
To save Israel from seventy years' bondage.

Because he came, we keep the Sabbath Day.
Because he came, we know the truth.
Because he came, we keep passover.
Our lives will never be the same because he came.[1]

Having presented a specific account of the life of the founding father of the Church of God and Saints of Christ, I will now examine the general development of the church. Insofar as I have already detailed the formation of the church in Lawrence, I will begin with what I am calling the movement's "eastern migration." Shortly after the church's first general assembly in Emporia, Kansas (June 24 , 1898) Crowdy headed northeast to Chicago. He arrived there in the fall of that year. Upon his arrival Crowdy took up the ministry that he had begun there in 1896. Additional churches were established and the movement's Chicago constituency grew. While there, Crowdy received a letter from a Mrs. Titus of Oneida, New York which contained the train fare to Oneida and a plea for him to come there and preach. Crowdy accepted the invitation and began his trek to the east.[2]

Crowdy's trip to Oneida was lengthy and indirect. Along the way he established churches in Detroit, Michigan, Armhurstburg, Ontario; and Syracuse, New York. The amount of time that was needed to accomplish this is not clear based on the best available data. It is known that Crowdy had arrived in Oneida and had begun an active ministry by March of 1899.[3]

While in Oneida, Crowdy's main activities were preaching and baptizing. He baptized over sixty people into the faith, many of whom were white. Once a sufficient number of people were gathered, Crowdy turned the pastoral duties over to George Labiel. He was the first ordained pastor of CGSC in the East. Crowdy moved on from there and began establishing churches in other New York towns. The list of places in which he planted churches includes Rome, Utica and New York City. While in New York City he baptized over 1000 individuals and formed a congregation larger than any previously established. This tabernacle was organized on May 6, 1899 under the leadership of Elder Mark Marsh.[4]

From here Crowdy returned to Lawrence to attend the first significant organizational meeting of the church (Oct. 10, 1899). Representatives came from Kansas, Illinois, New York, New Jersey, Missouri, Pennsylvania, Maryland, Texas, Colorado, Virginia, Nebraska, Michigan and Ontario. The most substantial product of this assembly was the establishment of a presbytery for four districts. The northwest district was headed by Elder Paul Hill. This district included Pennsylvania, New Jersey, Connecticut, Massachusetts, Vermont, New Hampshire, Maine, New York and Ontario. The southwestern district was headed by Elder J. H. Evans. This district included Missouri, Arkansas, Louisiana, Mississippi, Alabama, Tennessee, Kentucky, Virginia, West Virginia, North Carolina, South Carolina, Georgia and Florida. The northeastern district was headed by elder Gus William. This district included Wisconsin, Illinois, Indiana, Michigan and Ohio. The southeastern district was headed by Elder J. H. Brown. This district included California, Nevada, Utah, Arizona, New Mexico, Indian Territory, Texas, Washington, Idaho, Colorado, Oregon, Montana, Wyoming, North Dakota, South Dakota, Nebraska and Minnesota. This was an important event in that it demonstrated Crowdy's ability to organize a structure that was capable of being sustained beyond his life time. It similarly demonstrated the scope of his vision.[5]

Shortly after this meeting Crowdy left the West for good. He returned to the east and extended his ministry into Philadelphia. He remained in Philadelphia from 1900 until 1903. He first established residency on Pine street, near 11th. In the fall of 1901 he set up a printing press which published *The Weekly Prophet* under the guidance of Brothers Mansfield, Lynch and Edward Suydam. Soon thereafter he moved to 1626 Fitzwater and established his home there. Crowdy focused his ministry on outdoor preaching at the corner of Broad and Lombard. O'Neil Hall, which is located on this corner, later became the meeting place for the church's general assemblies. It also served as the location for the first passover celebration.[6]

Many of Crowdy's converts were recruited from other religious bodies. This enraged a Rev. Mr. Taliaferro and a Dr. Credit, two local pastors. They circulated a petition which demanded that Crowdy be run out of town. Their reason for doing so was that Crowdy advocated worship on Saturday. They presented the petition to the mayor of Philadelphia who refused to act without hearing Crowdy's side of the story. The mayor attended one of Crowdy's services and was impressed with his sincerity. He refused to expel Crowdy, stating that the city needed more individuals with his character and concern.[7]

Because of the length of Crowdy's stay in Philadelphia, the church grew to the unprecedented total of 1500 members. As a result of this it was necessary to move out of O'Neil Hall in order to accommodate the congregation. Evangelists Dickerson and Grimes located Quaker City Hall on Fitzwater and Broad which became the new location of the church. Here a celebration called "The Feast in the Wilderness" was held. Soon after this a passover called "Black Passover," because of the form of dress, was held.[8] While it was not the first Passover organized by the church it was by far the largest and most extensive. It was held on the 13th of April which continues to be the benchmark for setting the Passover date. The next two Passovers (1902 and 1903) were known as the purple Passovers, also because of the form of dress. These Passovers were characterized by the eating of lamb and two days of active celebration of the faith.[9]

In 1903 a Small Pox epidemic broke out in Philadelphia and took the lives of many of the church's members. Many feared that Crowdy would be consumed by this disease as well and encouraged him to leave the city. He consented to do so and in December of 1903 he took up residence in Washington D.C. on C street. Later, in the spring of 1904, me moved his residency to U street. While in the capital city he gave a great deal of consideration to the uniforms of the members and the functions of the church's choir. These thoughts were recorded and have been used to set standards that continue to be adhered to today. The most notable event during Crowdy's stay in Washington D.C. was a heavily attended celebratory march on September 24, 1905. In 1906 the "Plainfield Passover" was held. The blue and brown costumes used on this occasion established a tradition which the church has preserved. In the fall of 1907, Crowdy traveled to Newark, New Jersey where he suffered a stroke from which he failed to recover. Prior to his death Crowdy appointed Chief Joseph W. Crowdy (his nephew), Calvin S. Skinner and Bishop W.H. Plummer to be his successors. He died August 4, 1908 while in the care of his first wife and Malinda Morris.

J.W. Crowdy, C.S. Skinner and W.H. Plummer assumed important roles within the church. Crowdy became chief evangelist, the chief public speaker of the movement, with authority over all pulpits. Plummer became evangelist and "Grand Father Abraham"; this role included managing the business affairs of the church. Skinner became counselor of the church, an office which oversaw all counseling (major corporate decisions) activities in the church.

Joseph Wesley Crowdy was born Nov. 8, 1875. He first came in contact with his uncle W.S. Crowdy in 1899 while the latter was preaching in Maryland. J. W. Crowdy was inspired by his uncle's message and became one of his followers. In 1902, while in Washington D.C., J.W. Crowdy came into contact with another prominent figure in the organization, Evangelist John Dickerson. Under Dickerson's instruction he was sent to Philadelphia to become ordained Chief Evangelist of the CGSC by his uncle W.S. Crowdy. In the same year he was sent to Danville, Virginia and became the understudy of Evangelist Grimes. In 1903, W.S. Crowdy sent for J.W. Crowdy to head a tabernacle in Philadelphia. He there distinguished himself through his musical compositions and his biblical scholarship. In his capacity as evangelist he continued to establish churches in the United States and Africa. He died January 1, 1917 in Philadelphia.

William Henry Plummer was born in Montgomery County, Maryland on September 1, 1868. He was orphaned at an early age, leaving him with responsibilities above and beyond those of the average youth. The parentless Plummer sought guidance from elderly people in the community. Through his conversations with them he was encouraged to pursue an education which was believed to be a step towards liberation. Plummer soon went to Philadelphia, where greater educational opportunities existed. There he encountered W.S. Crowdy. Plummer contributed significantly to the development of the CGSC. He was the first chorister.[10] He also served as first superintendent of the sabbath school and later was ordained an elder in Jersey City, New Jersey. Before long he was appointed an evangelist and was transferred to Boston. While in Boston Plummer established a very large church that was distinguished by the musical element in its worship services. Plummer also had a keen business sense. In order to support himself and the church he began a small fruit stand which eventually grew into a complex of related enterprises including two grocery stores, a restaurant and a furniture store. Another of his accomplishments was the establishment of a Widows and Orphans home in Boston. It was in 1904 that he was appointed to the position of Grand Father Abraham, as well of general superintendent overseeing the church's business affairs. On February 12, 1917 Plummer was appointed Cardinal Bishop over the entire church, a role he held until his death on December 28, 1931.

During Plummer's tenure as the church's head he accomplished a number of feats that figured prominently in the organization's development. In 1901, W.S. Crowdy had purchased 40 acres of land in Belleville, Virginia. Plummer moved the headquarters of the CGSC to that site in 1917. In 1919 he established the Belleville Industrial School and Widows and Orphans Home. It was incorporated in 1921.[11] The home and school began in a two story frame building on the site in Belleville. Later improvements were made on the original building and dormitories were added. Further additions and improvements were made to facilitate the needs and activities of the church. These included a building for church services, additional classrooms, a residence for the president and his family, dining halls, a commissary, a printing plant, a blacksmith shop, garages, offices, farm buildings, a music hall and athletic fields. Today the property still has remnants of the music hall, offices, school, parsonage study, print shop, Widows and Orphans Home and an old tabernacle. Its primary function today is to provide low rent housing — a project that is sponsored by the church and is funded by the Department of Housing and Urban Development. Plans have been made to construct homes for the elderly on the property in the future.

Calvin S. Skinner was born February 16, 1847. He met Prophet Crowdy while he was preaching in Philadelphia in 1901. Skinner's most notable accomplishment within the organization was as a church builder. He established many tabernacles in the northeastern United States including ones at Wilmington, Delaware; Chester, Pennsylvania; Camden, New Jersey; and Trenton, New Jersey. During the passover of 1906, in Plainfield, N.J. he was appointed to the position of Counselor. He became the leader of the CGSC on December 22, 1931 when W.H. Plummer died. He held this position until his death on February 24, 1932.

Howard Zebulun Plummer was born on November 16, 1899 in Philadelphia, Pennsylvania, the son of W.H. Plummer and Mrs. Jennie B. Plummer. He attended elementary and high school in Boston, Mass., and then continued his studies at Massachusetts Institute of Technology. On April 20, 1917, he was ordained as an elder in Washington, D.C., at the age of seventeen. He was installed as Rabbi on December 28, 1931 and after Calvin S. Skinner's death became acting head in February of 1932. During his reign he aided in the project of the Belleville Industrial School and Widows and Orphans' Home.[12]

During his life he gave of his time and efforts to many an organization. He was a Trustee of Phi Beta Sigma Fraternity; a Charter Member of the Founders of Norfolk Polytechnic College, which is now Norfolk State College; held a life-time Gold Membership Card for the Hunton Branch Y.M.C.A. (from this organization he received on November 8, 1967 an award for outstanding contributions); and was a member of the Board of Directors, Organizer and Past President of Tidewater Chapter, Frontiers International; he was also President of the Interdenominational Interracial Hampton Ministers Conference. He organized the Masonic Lodge in Belleville, VA, known as the W.H. Plummer Lodge No. 271, and organized the Eastern Star Chapter known as Belleville Chapter No. 148. He was past Worshipful Master of Prince Hall Grand Lodge of the State of Virginia; Past Worshipful Master of W.H. Plummer Lodge 271; Past Grand High Priest of King Cyrus Grand Chapter Holy Royal Arch Masons of the State of Virginia; Past Commander of King Baldwin Grand Commandery, Knights Templar of the State of Virginia; Past Deputy of the Valley of Virginia for the United Supreme Council Scottish Rite Masonry; an active 33rd Degree Mason, Grand Master of Ceremonies and Grand Minister of the United Supreme Council of the Ancient Accepted Scottish Rite of the Southern Jurisdiction; Past Imperial Potentate and Imperial

Lecturer of the Ancient Egyptian Arabic Order Nobles of the Mystic Shrine of North and South America and its Jurisdiction. Also, on September 18, 1967, he received a "Merit of Honor" award for outstanding contributions to the development of youth in Virginia from the Order of the Knights of Pythagoras.[13] He died on February 24, 1980 leaving his son to take his place.

Levi Solomon Plummer was born on June 1, 1921. L.S. Plummer spent his early life in Boston, Massachusetts while attending English High School. Later he received his B.Sc. at New York University and his B.D. at Howard. He was ordained to the ministry in 1941 and served as Assistant Pastor in Boston, Mass., for three years. In 1944 he served in Washington, D.C. Plummer is a member of Frontiers International, a Thirty-two degree Mason, Ancient Egyptian Arabic order, Nobles of Mystic Shrine of North and South America, and various other civic functions. He was made a Bishop in 1953 and assisted his father (H.Z. Plummer) in an administrative capacity of the CGSC and the Belleville Industrial School and Widows and Orphans Home Inc. The following fifty-three tabernacles (plus seven others in South Africa) exist today under L. S. Plummer's jurisdiction:

Trenton, NJ — Elder George Abynathya

Chicago, IL — Elder Benjamin A. Byrd

Springfield, MA — Elder Charles Chamber

Charlotte, NC — Elder William Chese

Wilmington, DE — Elder Joseph B. Crisden

Philadelphia, PA — Rabbi Jehu A. Crowdy

Binghamton, NY — Elder Moses Cunningam

Jacksonville, FL — Elder Cecil R. Eaves

Boston, MA — Elder Jehu Eaves

Dorchester, MA — Elder Isaac Edwards

Portsmouth, VA — Elder Clifton C. Farrar

Mt. Vernon, NY — Elder Louis Gaskins

Richmond, VA — Elder Samuel Golson

Hartford, CT — Elder John R. Hall

Atlanta, GA — Elder Andrew Hart

Yonkers, NY — Elder David W. Hurt

Cumberland, MD — Elder F.T. Hurtt

Rochester, NY — Elder Joseph Jeffries

Johannesburg, South Africa — Elder Lameck Jiyane

Baltimore, MD — Elder Charles Johnson

Buffalo, NY — Elder Douglas Jordan

Hackensack, NJ — Elder Benjamin Keeling

Gary, IN — Elder Ewell G. Kent

Kingston, Jamaica, West Indies — Rabbi Hugh H. Levy

Rhodesia, South Africa — Elder Ambrose Makawaza

Uitenhage, South Africa — Elder Reuben Matshaka

Cincinatti,OH — Elder James McNeil

Detroit, MI — Elder Phillip Merritt

Washington, D.C. — Elder Jesse Monroe

Chicago, IL — Elder David Morrison

Zululand, South Africa — Elder Amom Mtembu

Salisbury, MD — Elder Wilmer Parker

Roanoke, VA — Elder Sherman C. Perdue

Greensboro, NC — Elder Curtis Person

Providence, RI — Elder Preston Mangana

Newark, NJ — Elder Benjamin Quattlebaum

Albany, NY — Elder Samuel Quattlebaum

Yonkers, NY — Elder G.B. Roberts

Plainfield, NJ — Elder Gideon Smith

New Haven, CT — Elder Jehu O. Smith

Canton, OH — Elder William C. Smith

Cleveland, OH — Rabbi William E. Stewart

Chester, PA — Elder Robert Tucker

Harrisburg, PA — Elder John Prince Walker

Los Angeles, CA — Rabbi H.W. Watson

Bridgeport, CT — Elder Harry Williams

Deland, FL — Elder James A. Williams

Atlantic City, NJ — Elder Harry N. Wilson

Toledo, OH — Elder Dewey Worthy

South Pines, NC — Elder D.J. Worthy

Norfolk, VA — Elder Charles D. Yancey

Alexandria, VA — Elder Ambrose Young

Gastonian, NC — Elder Arjamal Weathers[14]

The fact that there are only sixty tabernacles in 1988 when in 1936 there were 213[15] is more than likely due to the fact that in 1908 (right after William Saunders Crowdy died), the church split into two branches.[16] An account of these factions are as follows:[17]

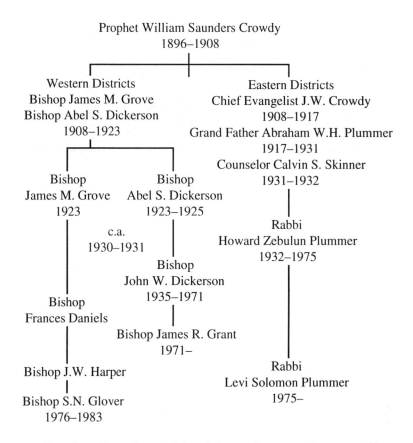

Prophet William Saunders Crowdy
1896–1908

Western Districts
Bishop James M. Grove
Bishop Abel S. Dickerson
1908–1923

Bishop
James M. Grove
1923

Bishop
Abel S. Dickerson
1923–1925

c.a.
1930–1931

Bishop
Frances Daniels

Bishop
John W. Dickerson
1935–1971

Bishop James R. Grant
1971–

Bishop J.W. Harper

Bishop S.N. Glover
1976–1983

Eastern Districts
Chief Evangelist J.W. Crowdy
1908–1917
Grand Father Abraham W.H. Plummer
1917–1931
Counselor Calvin S. Skinner
1931–1932

Rabbi
Howard Zebulun Plummer
1932–1975

Rabbi
Levi Solomon Plummer
1975–

Prophet Crowdy, in his visions, foresaw the spreading of the CGSC to black people all over the world. This prompted the organization to deploy an overseas missionary force. The two main targets became the West Indies and South Africa. Evangelist Howard L. Chase traveled to Jamaica to establish the CGSC there. He resided at the Levi home, 85 Windward Road, Kingston, for five years. While located here he baptized four adults and blessed four children. Later a building was rented at Regent Street which served as the Tabernacle. Here thirty-one were baptized and twenty-four children were blessed. This was also the location of the first holy convocation. Since then headquarters has been established at 59 East Queenstreet, Kingston. Today there are two churches in Jamaica.[18]

The ministry in South Africa was initiated by a Xhosa, Albert Christian, a sailor and former Baptist missionary, based in Port Elizabeth. While in Port Elizabeth Christian had a dream in which he purportedly received instructions to go to America and seek out Crowdy. He did so and returned to Africa in 1903 as a minister under Crowdy's charge. Christian founded churches first at New Brighton, Port Elizabeth, and Uitenhage and then throughout the Eastern Cape and as far north as the Transvaal. His successors were Samuel Matshaka, John Msikinya and Enoch Mgijima.[19]

I found no information on Matshaka and little information on Msikinya. What I know about Msikinya is gleaned from Dr. Oosthuizen's letter of Feb. 1 1988. Dr. Oosthuizen is my contact in Natal, South Africa. John J. Msikinya came in contact with the church at Lincoln University, the school he attended. He was born in 1867 at Fort Beaufort district and was originally a preacher in the Methodist church (before he was excommunicated). He returned to East Cape Uitenhage as bishop of Crowdy's church and established tabernacles in Peddie, Victoria East and Grahamstown. In 1909 the Cape Colony government became conscious of this church. Msikinya practiced baptism by immersion during the night (later only during the day). The peculiar rituals of the COGSOC was perceived as a threat to the state. Later reaction from the police led to the disappearance of the church in Peddie and Grahamstown. Msikinya moved his teachings to the Queenstown area and there emphasized that the COGSOC was established to help liberate blacks from their oppression. During this time period the end of the world was a dominate theme which promoted the selling of all personal wealth. Msikinya died in 1914 and Enoch Mgijima succeeded him.[20]

Now known as the Israelites, awaiting their promised land, Enoch Mgijima led the members of the church starting in 1912. Once a Mfengu peasant and Wesleyan lay preacher, Enoch shook the church with his visions of 1907 of an impending millennium. There were several black churches that Mgijima could have joined (i.e.: the African Presbyterian Church, the African Native Mission Church and the African Methodist Episcopal church) but he chose the COGSOC because of the tolerance for prophetic visions.

Mgijima knew quite a bit about W.S. Crowdy and his prophetic visions for the church. Upon joining the church he was informed that before Crowdy died (in 1908) he had established twelve tabernacles in South Africa. Mgijima was baptized at Kamastone by some of his followers in the Black Kei. It is known that Msikinya and Mgijima were rivals and when Mgijima died in 1914, Msikinya became bishop. During this time Enoch became noted in the region for his annual predictions of events (i.e.: automobile, flu epidemic of 1918, and the Bullhoek massacre). These prophecies, however, were minor elements in his message when compared to the major cataclysm which he envisaged.

Mgijima regarded his sect as an instrument of God's will, and in the final judgment, only the elect, his followers, were to achieve salvation and redemption. His concept of the elect was quite possibly derived from Crowdy's contention that blacks were descendants of the lost tribes of Israel for Mgijima claimed that his Israelites were direct descendants of two tribes, Judah and Benjamin. He may also have closely identified himself with the Biblical Israelited for he could draw many parallels between them and his own Hlubi ancestors. Both had similar ritual practices and social structures. Like the Israelites, his group had been forced into exile and had suffered many deprivations in their migrations before finding a home. However, Mgijima's Kamastone had not yet found a home.

In 1918 Enoch Mgijima was excommunicated from the COGSOC due to his visions. One of these visions represented a battle between two white Governments. In his vision he had seen a baboon crush these Governments and destroy them. The interpretation he put upon this was that the white Governments represented the Dutch and the English, and the baboon the Africans. This meant that the white people would be crushed by the natives.

During this period Mgijima gathered his people at Bullhoek (near Queenstown) and they formed a colony of 300 huts, erected on Crown land without permission. Mgijima's people, the Israelites, were warned twice that their group was not allowed to stay on Crown land. They never heeded the warnings. In 1918 over 117 of Mgijima's followers (excluding Mgijima) were killed by the machine guns of the government. This incident confirmed the governments suspicions of Native Separatist Churches and a task force was assigned to look into the incident (headed by a Dutch Reformed Church leader — Rev. P. VanderMerwe and Dr. C.T. Loram). It was decided that groups should be allowed to exist as long as they pose no threat to the government.[21]

From this one can see that the history of the church in South Africa leaves with it ties to the Bullhoek massacre. A sorrowful event in history of how easy it is for people to take the power positions they have been assigned and use it to the detriment of a people.

From a rather modest beginning in the heart of the midwest, the Church of God and Saints of Christ has, at one time or another, stretched from coast to coast in the United States and has extended abroad into the West Indies and South Africa. W.S. Crowdy's vision inspired this dispersion. His charismatic qualities have nourished and sustained the movement throughout its history. The account that I have just provided documents the breadth of the CGSC. In the section that follows, dealing with the church's theology, I will be documenting the spiritual depth of the group.

Notes

[1] *The Weekly Prophet*, February 19, 1988, No. 1204.

[2] Beersheba Crowdy Walker, *Life and Works of William Saunders Crowdy* (Philadelphia: Elfreth Walker, 1955) p. 23.

[3] *Oneida City Paper*, March, 1899. The document which states that Crowdy established the three churches mentioned is Walker, p. 24. This source is chronologically weak and as such I am unable to determine how much time was spent on the actual process of establishment and the degree to which Crowdy was active in this process.

[4] *Ibid.*, page 24.

[5] *Ibid.*, page 25.

[6] *Ibid.*, pages 27, 38.

[7] *Ibid.*, page 29.

[8] It was called Black Passover because everyone wore black and white.

[9] Walker, pp. 33, 41.

[10] The Chorister is the individual within the church who is responsible for the musical component of the worship procedure. This is a substantial role within the CGSC; music is central both to the theology and practice of their faith.

[11] Here is a list of the rules and guidelines mandated for individuals living at the home.

1. To establish, own, conduct and operate a school where students may obtain, on such terms and in such manner as may be deemed advisable and permitted by law, a general education and course of instruction in agriculture, business, trades and professions.

2. To establish, own, conduct and operate a widows and orphans home or homes for the care, maintenance and relief of indigent widows, orphans and other poor, needy, or homeless persons.

3. To acquire, take, hold and own all such property, both real and personal, including stocks and bonds of other corporations, as may be acquired by gift, purchase, devise or bequest, and use, operate, enjoy

and dispose of the same for its benefit in such manner as may be deemed advisable and permitted by law.

   4. To do any and all lawful acts and things whatsoever which may be incidental to or necessary for the accomplishment of the purpose hereinbefore mentioned.

   [12] The biographical data of the named persons comes from *A Brief History of the Department Sabbath School 1976* (Belleville: 1976), pp. 8–15.

   [13] I acquired this information by looking at an enclosed case that the headquarters in Virginia. had for H.Z. Plummer.

   [14] "1973 Directory," *The Weekly Prophet*, March 16, 1973, p. 2.

   [15] T.F. Murphy, *Census of Religious Bodies: 1936*, vol. 2, part one (Washington D.C.: U.S. Government Printing Office, 1941), p. 443.

   [16] E.J.P. Walker, *The Armour Bearer* (Philadelphia: E. Walker, 1961), p. 8. "Church of God — Bishops in Court." *Philadelphia Tribune*, June 28, 1913. Both of these articles tell about the court decision of 1913 that allowed for the split thus mentioned.

   [17] Sara Margaret Stone. *Transmission and Performance practice in an urban black denomination — The Church of God and Saints of Christ* (Kent State University, Ph.D., 1985), p. 126. Sara Stone studied the faction of the church known as the Western District. She did not label the districts Western and Eastern in her diagram, nor did she give the dates of the faction that this book centers on (the Eastern District).

   [18] *Church of God and Saints of Christ Directory. —* In Honor of our 50th Anniversary — 1946, pp. 237–239.

   [19] *Ibid.*, pg. 250.

   [20] From the letter of Prof. G.C. Oosthuizen of Natal, South Africa, February 1, 1988. Also from the "Daily Dispatch," June 8, 1920 – December 12, 1921.

   [21] *Enoch Mgijima, the Israelited Bulhoek Massacre, 1921* (Los Angeles: University of California Press, 1977), pp. 36–42.

Theological Description of the Church

The theological dimension of the Church of God and Saints of Christ is a powerful foundation for the church's normative beliefs and principles and socio-religious practices. It provides the constitution for a course of human emancipation and could easily be characterized as a liberation theology.[1] While the church has no systematically developed presentation of its theology there are a number of theologically significant documents available from which one can extract a theology. In this section of the paper I will provide a systematic account of the basic tenets of the organization's belief system.

The most rudimentary elements of the church's theology were provided by the visionary experiences of Prophet Crowdy. Crowdy was without doubt a man with vision. Obviously the factual content of the narrative generated to convey his vision is beyond verification. It might be, in fact, that the most visionary aspect of Crowdy's work was his use of narrative to communicate the message with which he was inspired. Having already described the purported visionary experience that is basic to the foundation of the church (see Chapter III), I would now like to reflect on its theological significance. While this interpretation is obviously subjective I think that it provides insight into what "vision" means for the CGSC.

Crowdy's visionary experiences give him great stature in the movement. Crowdy is regarded not merely as a great leader, great minister or great administrator, he was a prophet. The CGSC sees Crowdy as squarely within the prophetic tradition of the Old Testament. This tradition has

had a special meaning for blacks since their first exposure
to American religion (see Chapter II). The biblical stories
of a great prophet receiving a sign from God showing the
way out of oppression provided hope for blacks during the
period of slavery. By latching on to this tradition, Crowdy
had a historically pre-established bases for generating a
following with a liberation emphasis.[2]

Further, the claim of prophet status itself was helpful in
generating a following. American blacks at the turn of the
century were struggling with the problem of self-
determination (see Chapter I). Having spent many
generation under the domination of authoritarian master,
they found shifting into a situation where decision making
and self-motivation were part of the daily routine difficult.
Yet attaining these qualities was also basic to survival.
Crowdy, through the use of his visionary experience,
established a type of authority which, rather than
dominating and suppressing, sparked in his followers a
strong sense that they could achieve the things necessary to
survive in an environment where racism was the norm. The
inspiration came not so much from Crowdy, as from the
transcendentally inspired experience that marked him off as
a leader. Crowdy utilized the status attributed to him to
collect black people into religiously based communities
which provided the strength necessary for the people to
endure and overcome the hardships of the world in which
they lived.[3]

I would now like briefly to explicate some of the
significant aspects of Crowdy's initial vision (see Chapter
III). The vision begins with the startling image of tables
covered with vomit descending from the heavens. These
tables, Crowdy contended represented churches — the
Baptist church which had the largest black following was
the biggest and filthiest. The point this makes is that
existing religious bodies were sick. I would infer from this
that the disease infecting these groups is racism — the
illness that represents the greatest threat to a minority
attempting to establish an emancipated existence.

The next image is that of the white table descending, touching ground and then extending. It is purity that characterizes this table (or, if you will, social institution) — a purity of infinite capacity. This segment of the vision indicated the need to establish and perpetuate a movement of peoples committed to purifying a racially contaminated social structure. The truth of the "true church" suggests a true existential harmony which doesn't know the boundaries and limitations of bigoted pollution.

Finally, the vision includes a practical dimension. Crowdy receives a set of guidelines (the Seven Keys) which provide a concrete model for acting in the world. They have the additional benefit of being relatively vague, making them open to a number of interpretations as the spiritual and social consciousness of the church's members develops. In a sense, for Crowdy's vision to materialize to the fullest degree, everyone in the world would have to be a member of the church. If membership in the church simply requires a sense of spiritual unity that knows no racial barriers this is a provocative objective.

For the following reasons Crowdy's vision is the basis of the group's theology: **a)** It plugs the group into a very specific religious tradition; **b)** It indicts the corruption in existing religious institutions and posits a purified alternative; **c)** It provides the movement with a representation of authority without imposing authoritarianism; **d)** Finally, it offers the regulation that define it as a theology of praxis — liberating praxis. I will now proceed to account systematically for the theology that emerged from this foundation.

Another important, although officially unrecognized, aspect of the CGSC's theological constitution is the incorporation of rituals and practices that are derived from Prince Hall Masonry. Crowdy and many of his followers like H.Z. Plummer and L.S. Plummer were and are active masons. Guthrie was the center of Freemasonry in Oklahoma during the late 19th century.[4] It is clear that at one point Crowdy was heavily involved in Masonry.[5] As the first phases of his prophetic experiences began to take shape, however, he lost interest in the Masons.

> His wife thought this the result of too much carousing with his "brothers" whom she accused of making her husband drink when she was not at home, she asked him to give up his lodge meetings, for he was an ardent Mason, but he had really not attended his meetings in quite a while.[6]

The Masonic order did not cease to influence him. It is obvious that a number of themes central to Masonry carried over into Crowdy's development of the CGSC.

Sarah M. Stone, in her dissertation "Transmission and Performance Practice in an Urban Black Denomination — The Church of God and Saints of Christ," argues that it is the case that the formation of the CGSC was influenced significantly by Crowdy's Masonry. In my opinion, as well as Stone's, this is speculative. However, given the circumstances I feel that it is a plausible theory. Stone states that the rosettes, sashes, crowns, shepherds' staffs, belts and swords, bugles, mortar boards, various greetings, handshakes and marches are similar to grab and rituals in the Masonic order. She also cites symbols which are similar including the All Seeing Eye God, *The Stone of Truth*, *The Seven Keys* and the centrality of the color blue. Terms used by Crowdy that reflect a Masonic influence include Grand Officers and General Officers.[7] The importance of Masonry to Crowdy is signified by the Masonic symbol on his tombstone.[8] I make this point not to detract at all from the independent genius of the group's faith. It is clear that Crowdy was a religiously inspired individual. Religious inspiration, however, often draws upon aspects of everyday life and utilizes them in a vitally spiritual manner. This, to me, is the case with Crowdy's, and the CGSC's, appropriation of Masonic elements.

The final foundational element that I will briefly discuss in the literature that is basic to the group's formation. It is clear from the account that I have provided of Crowdy's vision that the Bible is the main document (see Chapter II). "And I took the little book out of the angel's hand and ate it up; and it was in my mouth sweet as homey: and as soon as I had eaten it, my belly was bitter . . . "[9] Crowdy was seen as having embodied the scripture in its entirety. It is important to note that this is compatible with the synthesis of Judaism and Christianity. The major literary sources of both traditions are present in the Bible.

Many major CGSC theological themes have heavily Jewish overtones. The first, and possibly the most important, is the theme of Exodus. As I mentioned above (see Chapter I), black people under slavery identified closely with the us narrative in the Old Testament. This carried over into the consciousness of Crowdy and has continued to be central to the teaching and works of the church. The main idea is that embondaged people, through self-determination and with the aid of God, can find liberation. This, in the tradition of Judaism, is not merely a salvation from the earthly state: it is a transformation of oppressed conditions.[10]

Another important Jewish theme that has developed in the church is the rabbinate. It is not clear when exactly the term "Rabbi" was instituted in the church. Crowdy did not use it himself. It is, however, a development that is consistent with the Crowdy's emphasis on the centrality of Judaism in the church's belief system.[11] The role of the Rabbi is pastoral. His (it presently is an exclusively male role) duties include opening services, opening the holy of holies and the ark, leading the congregation in responsive readings, acting as the source of theological authority and a counselor to his flock.[12]

Judaism has built into its theology an exceptionally strong concept of the extended family. This is rooted in the notion that God is the father of a specific family of people which has an ethnic source of identity. As I mentioned above (see Chapter I) this type of familial bonding was something that took place in the slave communities. It was not so much biological as situational and racial factors that determined family. Crowdy sought to tap into the force inherent in unified action by making a connection between the family of Israelites and the family of blacks. Important evidence to this effect is found in Crowdy's view that true Jews are black.[13] This familial theme is one that is virtually impossible to derive from a distinctly Christian faith. Christianity has a greater concern with establishing God's true family in an otherworldly dimension. In Christianity, one's family in this world is just as apt to confound as to support achievement of a position in the true family.[14] The CGSC here is nearer to the Jewish than to the Christian point of view.

The group's sacred rituals also have Jewish overtones. Crowdy insisted upon beginning worship on Friday night and extending it through Saturday.[15] This is in congruence with the Jewish observance of the Sabbath. Crowdy also initiated the tradition of having a Passover celebration. He participated in at least six of these. The passovers during Crowdy's era and today are very similar to those celebrated within traditional Judaism. In addition, the church also observes the Fast of Tebeth, also known as Holy Convocation. This was instigated by Crowdy in January, 1904.[16]

These are the Jewish elements that are basic to the group's system of belief. As I will make clear in my discussion of the Christian themes below, this is not pure Judaism. That would have been inappropriate to the conditions of the people Crowdy sought as followers (basically Christian in the orientation: see note 11). These themes, however, clearly distinguish the group from traditional Christianity. It is these theological rudiments that strengthen the position that holds this group to be the first example of black Judaism in America.

Christianity also plays an important role in the theology of the Church of God and Saints of Christ. W.S. Crowdy's early sermons provide ample evidence of the group's Christian orientation. The idea that Crowdy proclaimed most vigorously was that the day of prophecy had not passed.

> But the people will try to dodge the word by saying there are not any prophets now, or that they are all done away with. Then the question arises, who did away with them. Christ did not. (Matthew 5:17)[17]

By focusing on this point, Crowdy established two key components of the group's theology: First, the traditional Christian church is confused about its relationship to Judaism. Second, the continuity between Judaism and Christianity is becoming manifest in the CGSC — the "true" church.[18]

Crowdy also placed a great deal of importance on the person of Jesus. Jesus is touted as an advocate of racial equality. The proclamation, "Love thy neighbor as thyself," served both as a prescription for behaviour within the group and an indictment of the treatment that black people received from whites.

> Then Matthew 19:17 tells us, if we enter into Life, keep the commandments, and James 1:27 says, "Pure religion and undefiled before God and the Father is this, to visit the fatherless and the widows in their affliction, and keep himself unspotted from the world" and had the southern people who claim great reverence for the Lord Jesus Christ, who claims more sacredness in their services, and particularly introduce themselves as a characteristic of the pure doctrine of Christ and morality, had the seen those things which I spoke about above they would not have had time to formulate a plan of Jim-crow separation nor for barbecuing men and women of the colored races; for if the loved God with all their hearts, and with all their mind, soul and strength, they could not help from seeing

the second commandment, which Christ says is
like unto it, "Thou shalt love thy neighbor as
thyself." (Mark 12:30–31)[19]

The important points that Crowdy makes in this statement
are two: that Jesus in the subjective role model for
establishing a truly non-discriminatory existence; and that
the established Christian churches misrepresent.

Another theme that Crowdy drew from the Gospel
tradition provides the ethical direction for the group. It is
important to note that Crowdy did not promote a rigid
Jewish moralism. Nor did he advocate its Christian
counterpart, e.g. as found in the Deutero-Pauline letters.
Rather, the ethical standards of the group are drawn directly
from the life and teachings of Jesus.

The scripture says when you are converted old
things passed away. Now if you are converted,
leave lying, whoremongering, idolatry,
witchcraft, hoodooing, and all manner of isms,
you want to leave that behind and take up the
new things of Jesus Christ which by no means
will supper to do any of those things. I want
members to stop evil speaking of one another,
and don't care to undermine on another and let
me know it, if you can't speak a good word for
your neighbor, even if he is a sinner, hold your
peace [sic].[20]

The main moral theme that is developed by Crowdy, one
which relies heavily on Jesus' teachings, is that it is
imperative to treat others and oneself with dignity and
respect. This, one can infer, he viewed to be the foundation
of a doctrine of salvation from human oppression.

In general, Crowdy appropriated Christian thought to
the extent that it served the liberation objectives of the
group. A number of themes like salvation, brotherhood,
sisterhood, and renewal, etc. support these objectives. The

opening remarks of the Church's constitution provide a statement as to the group's relationship to Christianity.

> We, the Church of God and Saints of Christ, of the United States, and it jurisdiction do declare every person members of the Church of God, after having repented of their sins and being baptized by burial into the water, upon confession of faith in Christ Jesus, and received the unleavened bread and water for Christ's body and blood and their feet washed by the Elder as written in John 13:1–23, having agreed to keep the Ten Commandments and having been breathed upon with an Holy Kiss, also being taught how to pray as it is written, Matthew 6:9–13. We do try to perpetuate a union among the Saints of Christ and maintain a correspondence with all other Churches of God throughout the United States and the whole world. We therefore purpose to maintain and keep the Commandments of God and the sayings of Jesus according to the doctrine of the Bible.[21]

It can be inferred from this, as well as from the historical development of the group, that at the center of the Christian dimension of the church's theology is something of a social gospel.[22] The causes that Jesus struggled for — emancipation and redemption — have been those of American blacks up to this day. Crowdy preached Christian themes that are supportive of this cause; the ensuing leaders and the community of believers have retained and developed these themes into a civil rights-oriented form of Christian humanism.

The formal theology of the Church is found primarily in the Seven Keys and the Constitution. A summary of the church's constitution is as follows:

Believing that the Negro race is descended from the 10 lost tribes of Israel, the prophet taught that the Ten Commandments and a literal adherence to the teachings of the Bible, including both the Old and the New Testaments, are man's positive guides to salvation. In order, however, that the faithful may make no mistake as to the commandments which they are to follow, a pamphlet has been published by the church under the direction of the prophet called the "Seven Keys," which includes Bible references giving the authority for the various customs and orders of the church. Among these customs are the observance of the Jewish calender and feast days, especially the Jewish Sabbath, and the use of the corresponding Hebrew names.[23]

The Seven Keys are:

1. The Church of God and the Saints of Christ.
2. Wine forbidden to be drunk in the Church of God forever.
3. Unleaven bread and water for Christ's body and blood.
4. Foot washing is a commandment.
5. The disciples prayer.
6. You must be breathed upon with a Holy Kiss.
7. The Ten Commandments.[24]

The final main formal document is *The Bible Gospel Told: The Revelation of God Revealed* by W.S. Crowdy. This book tells the major tenets of the church, presented in question form with responding answers, like a catechism. It deals with subjects such as religion as a duty, dealing with hypocrisy, envy and jealousy, selfishness, repentance, footwashing, disciples prayer, etc. These sources provide the basis for the group's belief system. In the next chapter, I will deal with the way that the belief system affects the church's social organization and interrelation.

Notes

¹ The term liberation theology is most often associated with Catholic movements in Latin America where Christian theological themes are reconciled with Marxist praxis philosophy. This term has more recently been applied to theologies which are concerned with emancipation in other contexts, e.g. black theology, feminist theology of the CGSC because one of the central themes is improvement of the participants' condition in this world through a process of liberation from bondage.

² I don't think that the point can be made too emphatically that Crowdy was interested in returning, to the degree that it was possible, to the Jewish roots of the Christian faith. The simple reason for this is that the Jewish themes of bondage and liberation were appropriate to the condition of blacks at the time. It is worth noting here that Crowdy seemed to have a rather acute understanding of the pivotal point in history that blacks occupied. He knew that if something weren't done soon that it might be too late for the blacks of his time period to find liberation. This statement comes out of what I have read in the various sermons of Crowdy's. This further explains the urgency which directed his message.

³ It is worth noting again in this context that Crowdy established means for making a living as well as churches (see chapter III). The pattern that this established is one that has been carried over into the Belleville project (see chapter IV).

⁴ William H. Grimshaw, *Official History of Free Masonry Among the Colored People in North America* (New York: Broadway Publishing Company, 1969), p. 295.

⁵ Prince Hall Masonry was the only form of "lodge organization" open to blacks at this time. Prince Hall Masonry was founded in 1784.

Prince Hall was a radical black activist as well as a minister. He formed the organization for the purpose of building up the black community (he fought for equality before the law, education for black children, participation in the government, the right not to be publicly insulted and of course the abolition of slavery). While the degree of knowledge that Crowdy had of Prince Hall is not clear, one can speculate that he knew something of his character and vision. Crowdy possibly used him as a role model. See George W. Crawford, *Prince Hall and His Followers* (New York: AMS Press Inc., 1971), pp. 13–19.

[6] Beersheba Crowdy Walker, *Life and Works of William Saunder Crowdy* (Philadelphia: Elfreth Walker, 1955), p. 5.

[7] Sara M. Stone, "Transmission and Performance Practice in an Urban Black Denomination — The Church of God and Saints of Christ" (Kent State University, Ph.D. dissertation, 1985), pp. 426–430. It should also be noted that this dissertation focuses on music of the Dickerson faction which is not the faction of which I am doing a history. The faction which I am studying is the Crowdy/Plummer faction.

[8] I discovered this on a recent trip to the headquarters of the CGSC in Belleville, Virginia. The tombstone has a bird on a column which has two heads and a crown in the center. The bird looks like either an eagle or a hawk. I was informed by Elder Ezra L. Locke that this is a Masonic symbol.

[9] Walker, p. 3

[10] Crowdy was the liberator of the embondaged blacks who composed his following. The efforts to emancipate blacks from oppressed conditions has become a tradition in the ministry of the CGSC. See Jesse E. Brown's discussion in *Prophet William Saunders Crowdy and the Church of God and Saints of Christ: The Implications of his life and thought for the mission of the church* (Rochester: Colgate Rochester Divinity School, 1986), pp. 126–127.

[11] A theory which was suggested to me by a member of the organization who wishes to remain anonymous is that Crowdy was reserved in his use of Jewish language for fear that his followers, who were indoctrinated with Christianity — the religion of the White slave owners — would not identify with it. He nevertheless set Jewish precedents that have evolved into an increasingly Jewish theological orientation.

[12] *Ceremonies for Sabbath, High Holy Days and Festivals*, p. 12.

13 *Prophet W.S. Crowdy's Great Prophetic Sermons*, p. 9.

14 Quote the Bible verse.

15 Walker, p. 39.

16 Brown, p. 112.

17 W.S. Crowdy, *The Bible Gospel Told: The Revelation of God Revealed* (Washington: Church of God and Saints of Christ, 1902), p. 6.

18 The synthesis of these two traditions without qualifying the superiority of one over the other has a somewhat universalistic tone. Some segments of the group today view universalism to be the natural development of Crowdy's idea of the "true" church.

19 Crowdy, p. 24.

20 *Ibid.*, p. 24.

21 *The Constitution of the Church of God and Saints of Christ for the Grand Assembly of the United States* (1949 revision), p. 1.

22 For a good general description of the social gospel movement see Sydney Ahlstrom's, *Theology in America: The Major Protestant Voices from Puritanism to Neo-Orthodoxy* (New York: Bobbs-Merrill Co. Inc., 1967), pp. 531–587.

23 T.F. Murphy, *Census of Religious Bodies: 1936*, vol. 2, part 1 (Washington D.C.: U.S. Government Printing Office, 1941), p. 439.

24 *The Constitution Laws and Minutes* (Lawrence, Kansas: n.p., October 10, 1899), p. 8.

Social Dynamics of the Contemporary Church

Because He Came

God sent a man, his name was Crowdy
He came to bring back the ancient of days.
He said he just got down in time.
To save Israel from 70 years of bondage.

Because he came, we keep the Sabbath Day
Because he came, we know the truth
Because he came, we keep Passover
Our lives will never be the same
because he came.

Because he came, we have the Seven Keys,
One Hundred One Sayings and Uniforms,
And when he left he did not leave us comfortless,
Because he left with us Grand Father Abraham

Because he came, we keep the Holy Days,
Yom Kippur, and Succoth too,
We keep the New Year of Exodus 12:2,
And the days found in Leviticus 23.

Composed by Evang. C.C. Farrar, Nov. 5, 1987

Throughout this work I have alluded to the social implications of The Church of God and Saints of Christ. The church's early formation period was directly attached to a social movement: the liberation of southern slaves. The church's history is rich with examples of individuals that accepted the burden of promoting freedom and liberation for blacks in the early and middle 20th century. They have a theological foundation that reflects a process of thematization directed at altering the human condition in accord with divine ordinance. As a result of this progressive activist bent, the internal social dynamics of the church are models of power through unity. The concept which underlies this unity is the extended family. In the case of the CGSC the criterion for inclusion within the parameters of extension is a spiritual, rather than physical, commonality.

Given the amount of information available, one can best provide an inferential description of the micro-social dynamics of the specific congregations at various stages of the Church's development. These limitations do not apply to the contemporary Church. There are a number of active congregations in existence, each living out the visions of W.S. Crowdy in its own unique way. In the section that follows I will detail a typical weekend of worship for the CGSC based on two congregations that I have had the opportunity to observe first hand. I will focus on the way that the order of worship serves to constitute a bond of commonality that can be carried over into the affairs of the week. Insofar as the two churches that I have observed represent the socio-economic poles within the organization I will conclude this section with an analysis of the differences that are manifest due to this. The data compiled for this section are limited to information that I have gained through informal contact with church members. Hence my analysis will be more phenomenological than statistical.

The CGSC Sabbath is structurally quite similar to that of more traditional Jewish bodies. It begins on Friday evening and extends through Saturday. During this period two formal services are held through which a sense of spiritual unity is established and maintained. It is the corporate recognition of their mission and W.S. Crowdy that is at the forefront of the consciousness of individual members during the Sabbath.

The first formal gathering is on Friday evening. It serves to reinforce the sense of commonality and to fortify the web of extension. This is accomplished through periods of fellowship intermingled with prayer, teaching (sermons, etc.), and intense singing. The time spent in song seems to have a cathartic effect, releasing members from the distractions which separate them in order to gather them under the rubric of consciousness that makes them one. The order of worship is provided in Appendix I.

The Friday evening service is in general a less formal preparation for the day of intense activity that will follow. Church members are reunited through a worship procedure which encourages them to reflect on their common roots. This sets the stage for the next day's dramatic worship-celebration.

On Saturday morning members begin to arrive at the church around 8:30 a.m.. They spend some time in informal fellowship prior to the advent of the service. At 9:00 all members collect in a hall adjacent to the sanctuary for a time of singing together. This is the first moment of Sabbath day unison — an important collective event prior to the time when individuals and subgroups retire to activities that pertain specifically to their respective needs and concerns. For most this entails going to Sabbath school. The purpose of the Sabbath school program is to provide basic teaching as well as specific training. Members of the CGSC are strongly committed to this program. They feel that the future of the group is ensured through the training provided for the entire range of age groups. Some of the specific things that are taught in Sabbath school include basic knowledge of the Bible, knowledge of the teachings of Prophet Crowdy, the theology and doctrine of the church and the organization's historical development. While in Rhode Island, I had the opportunity to sit in on a children's Sabbath School class. The main focus was to educate the children about the stories of the Bible. This process starts at the young age of five or six. The class is led by a male Sabbath School teacher who enforces discipline and memorization of basic information gleaned from the scripture readings. During my visit to

Temple Beth El (in Virginia) the adult Sabbath school class discussed the battle between the Midianites and the Amalekites. This is an Old Testament story taken from II Samuel 12 & 13 and Judges 7–8. The main focus seemed to be on the ability to read clearly and with theatricalism. After a half hour of reading, three basic questions were asked by the Sabbath School teacher: **1)** What two tests were the soldiers subjected to? **2)** How did the Lord show Gideon that the battle was won? **3)** Was Gideon's Actions justified? If so why? Many of the members, regardless of gender or age, partook readily in the discussion, which was led by a male Sabbath School teacher. It was an informative hour.

The Sabbath School Manual is diverse in content. There is a list of "A Child's Ten Commandments," "The Ten Commandments of How to Get Along With People," hints to housekeepers and relevant information on first aid treatment. The piece of information that I find extremely valuable is the set of eighty-five black history questions that the church compiled from the *Black Collegian*. (See Appendix 2). When Sabbath school adjourns everyone gathers in a common hall for a light breakfast together. Here members have the opportunity to catch up on the details of each other's lives while sharing food together. Eating together is in effect, for the CGSC, an informal sacrament. It reminds the congregation of its interdependence, that the nourishment received is for both physical and spiritual (the relationship with each other and with the divine) vitality.

When this important time together comes to a close the members migrate to the sanctuary for the formal service. Time spent in the sanctuary begins with singing. The emotional state of members during this period ranges from deep solemnity to what could almost be described as ecstasy. Songs are sung that deal with topics such as the importance of Prophet Crowdy, the majesty of God, the path to freedom and the unity of the religious body. All of the music is sung under the direction of the head cantor. His/Her task is to select the appropriate songs and to lead the congregation in singing them. The songs, all original compositions by church members, are quite complex with three or four harmonic parts. All of the members know their parts and have the words secured in their memory. Throughout the song service members engage in various forms of marching which range from gently shuffling in place to forming lines and parading around the sanctuary. It was clear to me through my observations that the time of singing is one of the most important components of the religious experience for CGSC members. Following the singing, the most dramatic ritual of the service takes place: the Holy of Holies is opened. The Holy of Holies is what can best be described as a sacred cupboard (also known as the Ark of the Covenant) where the Torah is kept. It is slowly opened by the Rabbi and an Elder while the congregation slowly sings an appropriate song in the background. This ritual represents revelation. The precedent singing provided the necessary condition for receiving what was to be revealed. The next phase in the service develops the theme of revelation that has been developed. The final step, the sermon, completes the circle of revelation. Up to this point there has been a period of preparation and the source of revelation has been exposed or made explicit. A gap remains, however, between the source and those to whom revelation pertains. It is the role of the pastor to bridge that gap, to communicatively traverse the distance between truth and the recipient of truth. The content of the sermon varies greatly from congregation to congregation, and within a congregation from season to season. The model, however, for this revelatory sequence remains constant: it is a communal recreation of the visionary experiences of W.S. Crowdy.

When the message has been transmitted and received the Holy of Holies is ceremoniously closed (the opening procedure is reversed). This is followed by an "altar call" of sorts during which the "lost" are called back into the "fold" and new members are received. The service concludes with a closing song, a prayer of dismissal and the benediction. Each of these elements (song, prayer and declaration) expresses a similar message: encouragement to the membership to maintain the common and spiritual unity achieved during the Sabbath (See Appendix III).

The Sabbath is brought to an end with a large meal which all of the members take together. Here again there is an informal sacramental atmosphere. The meal begins at approximately 3:30 and runs into the evening hours. All the food is prepared and served by members of the congregation. In a sense the meal is an implicit commissioning service. Now that all are well fed (both spiritually and physically) they are adequately equipped to resume their roles in the secular world.

Several basic material elements play an important symbolic role in the life of the CGSC. The tabernacle configuration is relatively uniform from congregation to congregation. The pulpit is centrally located at the front of the church, on an elevated stage, along with several chairs for the pastor, elders and anyone else that will be speaking during the service. On the floor in front of the stage is a chair for the Sister Elder. To the left and right of this are semi-circular rows of chairs for the choir. On the far right end of the choir area is a seat for the Shepherd's Boy. At the far right side of the stage are chairs for deacons. The congregation, which sits facing the stage, is split down the middle by a broad aisle. The choristers' podium is located at the stage end of this aisle. The symbolically significant adornments that can be found in every sanctuary include the Ten Commandments either painted or enframed on the wall behind the stage, a picture of Crowdy and past elders or evangelists on either side wall, and often, a blue tapestry with the initials "C of G and S of C," the all seeing eye and the church's motto, "Stone of Truth" embroidered on it in gold.

The dress code adhered to by all members on the Sabbath is similarly important. The following set of standards must be meticulously followed. The men wear brown English walking suits, with high collars, bow tie, with a rosette on the lapel and a small metal-fanned badge, with a photograph of Crowdy. The women wear brown pleated skirts, blue blouses and brown ties with a photograph of Crowdy in the middle of the tie. In the summer, on the Sabbath, all the men wear white suits and white shoes, and the women wear white dresses, together with the ties, rosettes and badges mentioned. The dress regulations for other festivals and occasions are as follows:

Females

Black skirt with matching fabric belts	1)Beginning of Sabbath
White waist with white collar	2)Sunday Service
Black Bow in hair	3)Holy Convocation
Black oxford shoes	4)Re-establishment Day
Black shade hosiery	
White gloves	

Brown pleated skirt	1)Sabbath Day
Blue waist with matching fabric belts	2)Passover*
White collar	
Black oxford shoes	
Dark shaded stockings	
Church rosette	
White gloves	
*Sash	

Summer Uniform (Sabbath Day)

White shirt waist dresses
White shoes
Blue bow (on front of dress)
Blue fabric belt (to match bow)
Blue bow in hair
Church rosette
Stockings
White gloves

Males

Black formal suit with tails, high white collars	1)Beginning of the Sabbath
Black bow tie	2)Sunday Service
White vest	
Black pattern leather shoes	3)Holy Convocation
Black socks	4)Re-establishment Day
White gloves	

Brown English walking suit with high white collars	1)Sabbath Day
Brown Bow tie	2)Passover
White vest	3)Last Day of Holy Convocation

Black patent leather shoes
Brown socks
Church Rosette
White gloves

*Sash and three corner hat
**The men always wear a Tallit (prayer garment) and a Yarmulke (skull cap).

Summer Uniform (Sabbath day)

White suits, white shoes, white collar, brown tie, brown socks, church rosette and white gloves.[1]

There are many different symbolic meanings for the style and color of the dress. The blue represents the sky, brown the earth, white is light, purity, joy, and glory. They also wear ribbons in a variety of colors. The yellow signifies charity, honor and loyalty; pink is royalty; red is fire, blood, work, bravery, and courage; purple is sorrow, suffering, high rank and royalty; green is nature and eternal life; black signifies that the Lord dwells in thick darkness. Also of significance is that the blouse has 72 tucks which represent the 70 elders of Israel plus Moses and Aaron. The brown skirt has 52 pleats which represent the 52 weeks in the year.

The collar is stiff to remind the members of the stiffheartedness of the Children of Israel.[2]

The history of this dress code can be traced directly back to Crowdy. Two rationales were provided in defense of the dress code: **1)** It ensured that everyone would be discreetly dressed so that no one would be distracted during the service by thoughts pertaining to "the flesh"; **2)** By standardizing the mode of dress there would be no distinction between members based on something as superficial as clothing. Not only each article of clothing, but each component of each article has some representative significance. Here again the underlying purpose for insisting on uniform clothing is to set the group apart as a body of people and to avoid anything (such as jealousy and competition over clothing) that could weaken this sense of commonness.

Holidays play an important role in the social life of the church. The three primary holidays are Passover, Holy Convocation and Reestablishment day. Passover is a grand pilgrimage (See Appendix IV). All members that are able travel to the church's headquarters in Virginia to celebrate the Passover together. This takes approximately a week and serves a function similar to that of the weekly meeting, only on a much broader scale: it renews the sense of family among the membership at large and commissions them to act on the vision of their prophet. The link between past and present is achieved by bridging the generation gaps in the form of Passover seder in which the head of the religious family recounts the story of the Exodus from Egypt so that the younger generation can identify with and feel that he/she personally departed from Egypt. This is also achieved in the hymns, testimonies, sermons, and prayer.[3]

Holy Convocation is the Fast of the Tenth Month Tebeth. This holiday occurs in the holy week (towards the end of December) called Holy Days or Holy Convocation. The week begins with the blowing of trumpets at sundown at the close of the third day of Tebeth, and it ends with a feast on the tenth day. The members commemorate the Destruction of Jerusalem in approximately 586 B.C.E. by the Babylonians. Thus,these are days when individuals prepare themselves mentally and spiritually to live free from sin and full of love. Testimonies of thankfulness to God for His goodness are given and much thought is given to prayer. The prayers are to petition God for more love for themselves and their family and friends. Strict praying positions are adhered to at six in the morning. On the first day one is to sit in a chair with the head bowed; the second day one must stand erect, hands at side and head bowed; the third day one must sit in a chair, elbows on knees, face in hands; the fourth day one is to kneel on the floor, resting hands on a chair and face in hands; the fifth day one is to kneel with hands resting on the floor and face in hands; the sixth day one is to lie straight out on the floor with face in hands; the seventh day is the Feast day and all are to stand erect.[4] These different praying positions are important because they convey the idea that regardless of one's place in life one can pray to God and ask for forgiveness.

Re-Establishment Day is simply the day that is set aside to remember Prophet William Saunders Crowdy and to be re-educated about various historical facts of the movement. This event takes place on November eighth, the recognized starting date of the movement.

The other holidays are Rosh Hashanah, the Jewish New Year; Yom Kippur, is the day of atonement which is marked by fasting from sundown to sundown; Succoth (Sukkot), the Jewish harvest festival, occurring five days after Yom Kippur; Shavuouth, on the sixth of Sivan (seven weeks after Passover) in honor of the giving of the Ten Commandments; and Thanksgiving Day, a time to give thanks to God for all blessings.

The descriptions and interpretations that I have just provided are common to specific congregations of the CGSC. There are also some rather dramatic differences among the congregations. Some lean more towards Judaism than others. Some are very close to typical black Christian churches. Their theological basis is essentially the same but the way that individual churches interpret this can vary quite a bit. Through my discussions and observations I have tentatively concluded that a primary factor in the way that a specific congregation practices the theology of the CGSC is the socio-economic status of the members. I will provide evidence to this effect by describing the similarities and differences between the two churches that I directly observed: the church in Providence, Rhode Island and the church in Bellevue (Portsmouth), Virginia.

The church in Providence can be classified in terms of its geographical location: inner city urban. The socio-economic status of its membership reflected this. Most members were struggling to make ends meet. Many lived in housing projects within walking distance of the church. The immediacy of social problems faced by blacks had the effect of stimulating their political awareness. They translated the language of Crowdy's message into that of social activism.

The church in Belleville likewise can be classified in terms of its geographical location: middle class suburbia. Members of this congregation maintained a considerably higher standard of living. Their relationship to fellow "saints" living under less desirable conditions was limited. As such, their political consciousness was less informed by the urgency of the need for change. This in turn shaped the group's social behavior. The Belleville Church tended to focus on its own functioning; the Providence congregation was more cause-oriented. I will discuss the way that this was manifest in terms of three phenomena: the content of sermons preached, the observable degree of unity within congregations and the apparent quality of life of CGSC members.

The sermon preached in the Rhode Island church used an allegorical form to present a social-political message. Spiritual renewal was emphasized as a condition for improving the conditions of the black membership in this ghetto like community. The speaker drew an analogy between the conditions faced by post-abolition followers of Crowdy and contemporary members of the CGSC. Crowdy provided, for his followers, a spiritual vitality that enabled them to overcome many of the hardships which they faced. The same prescription was suggested for the contemporary membership. When a spiritually linked body acts, the difficulties created by the socio-economic situation of urban blacks can be transcended.

The focus of the sermon in Virginia was upon the women's group (namely the Daughters of Jerusalem and Sisters of Mercy) that has been a vital part of the organization. An emphasis was placed upon the functions and activities of that organization. In contrast to the vital call to action that was made at Providence, the emphasis was placed on the historical tradition of the "Daughters of Jerusalem" and the way that this tradition could best be preserved. The primary concern was maintenance or refinement, not transformation.

Unity among members played an important role in the lives of all involved in the Rhode Island church. The data that confirm this are based mainly on observation and discussion with individuals in the congregation. Relations among members were similar to those of family members. They were intimately involved in each other's lives and extended the fellowship experienced during the worship service beyond the doors of the church. I attribute this great intimacy to three things: **1)** The fact that this group was quite small facilitated close relationships; **2)** The religious experience for Rhode Island members was not so much a part of their heritage as a source of day to day nurture; **3)** The socio-economic conditions faced by the members meant a shared necessity for maintaining an adequate standard of living.

The unity of the Virginia congregation was also familial. The most striking differences that I observed was in the amount of wealth that individual members (or families) possessed and the size of the congregation. The economic differences enabled members to live more autonomously; the difference in size restricted intimacy. As such, the strong sense of community that I sensed in the Rhode Island tabernacle was not as apparent in Virginia. While the two groups shared a similar heritage and general theological orientation, the differences were striking. The spirituality in the Providence church was a lived spirituality. Discovering the essence of the divine, as manifested through the human, was perceived to be the catalyst for the movement from an intolerable past to a pivotal present and on toward a fully liberated future. Spirituality for the people in Virginia was a component of their own quest for emancipation — a process that is essentially complete. This is not to say that the spirituality of the Virginia body was dead; it simply played a less urgent role in the day to day existence of the member.

Notes

[1] Jesse E. Brown, "Prophet W.S. Crowdy and the Church of God and Saints of Christ: The Implications of his Life and Thought for the mission of the church" (Rochester: Colgate Rochester Divinity School, 1986), p. 142.

[2] Taken from a church handout entitled *Uniforms*.

[3] Jesse E. Brown, pp. 44–47.

[4] Taken from a church memo from Levi S. Plummer on November 12, 1987.

The Role of Women in the Church of God and Saints of Christ

Daughter's Song

Sing oh Daughters of Zion shout oh Israel, shout
    rejoice and be glad (repeated twice)
There is a prophet in the land, he is teaching the ten
commands. Rejoice and be glad. Our father will be
pleased children stay in the "seven keys" rejoice and
be glad.

(Manual of Daughters of Jerusalem, 1948)

The Daughters of Jerusalem is the organization within the CGSC in which women exercise their roles as leaders. It was founded June 26, 1898 in Emporia, Kansas by W. S. Crowdy. The original purpose of the group was to meet the physical needs of members incapable of caring for themselves. Several committees took care of such needs: **1)** The Look-Out Committee which cared for traveling ministers and congregation members; **2)** The Sick Committee visited and cared for the sick; **3)** The Ways and Means Committee looked after the minister's house and cared for the church's poor; **4)** The Widows and Orphans Committee saw to it that widows and orphans had the necessities of life; **5)** The Baptism committee; **6)** The Pulpit Committee looks after the basin for washing feet, makes sure the pastor has water during the sermon, keeps all articles around the pulpit clean; **7)** The Pastor's Table Committee collects a silver offering from each member and turns it over to the pastor's wife, taking the name and amount of each person contributing and sees that the pastor's table has a nice linen tablecloth and adequate refreshments for the Sabbath; **8)** The Pastor's Clothing Committee makes certain that the pastor is appropriately attired; **9)** Board of Trustees looked after the financial management of "The Daughters"; **10)** The Storehouse Committee maintained the stock of food and clothing necessary for conducting the functions of the other committees.[1] Women from the beginning played an important role in the organization. They cared for the sick, provided the family-like link among all members and ministered to the specific needs and hardships faced by black families.

In addition to these specific committee functions the Daughters of Jerusalem were also responsible for purchasing and/or making the uniforms (i.e. badges, ribbons, hairpieces), keeping records (i.e. births, deaths, weddings, etc.), and the rituals of the church services (i.e. funeral processions, mourning, footwashing, blessing of children, children's programs, junior quorums). They also published *The Daughters Newsletter* (published monthly beginning in 1948) which contained updates on the social life of the church as well as hints and tips concerning the operations of the home.

The following diagram outlines the structure of the organization:

Grand Father Abraham

This is the person who officially opens and closes meetings. This person also is the head of the church and usually delegates this position to another male member known as:

District Father Abraham

Assistant District Father Abraham

Grand Mother Sarah

This is the title given to the highest woman of the Daughters. She sets up local auxiliaries in the places where tabernacles exist and installs officers there. Her word is final and can be

suspended by no one but Grand Father Abraham. She also
sets the times for meetings, receives credentials of delegates,
appoints any committees necessary for various functions,
upholds laws of the organization and makes a report to the
Bishop annually.

Grand Rachel
She is the right hand support of Grand Mother Sarah. She
must travel and assist her in the work of the Daughters. If
Grand Mother Sarah could not attend a meeting Grand
Rachel would preside.

Assistant Grand Rachel
She carries out all the work and duties of the Grand Rachel
in the absence of the former.

Grand Leah
She is the left hand support of Grand Mother Sarah.

Grand Mary
She is the secretary of the organization. She receives all
monies, orders, collections, etc. She must also make an
annual report.

Assistant Grand Secretary
All official correspondence is her duty. She is also an
assistant to Grand Mary.

Grand Martha, Treasurer
Also known as the "bagholder," it is her duty to hold and
keep track of all funds. Annually she is to make a written
report of the financial situation of the organization.

Grand Storehouse Mistress
Fulfills the duties of head clerk. She is in charge of all the
storehouses which provide the Sabbath attire for the church
body.

Mother Exhorter

She is the counselor of the organization. She is empowered to instruct the Daughters on all matters pertaining to their welfare, best interests and duties. Any problems that a Daughter would have should be addressed to Mother Exhorter.[2]

Although this is not indicated in the above diagram (which represents the structure as it stands today), during the Crowdy era the leadership responsibilities held by women were tremendous. Women were frequently placed in pastoral roles. Two examples of this are Belle Slaughter and Elder Lavender.[3] Slaughter's role was as a street preacher in New York at the turn of the century. Lavender headed a congregation in Utica, New York. Both of these women were trained and inspired by Crowdy. These individuals serve as venerable role models for women engaged in the vital functions of the church.

The importance of the Daughters of Jerusalem was demonstrated during the celebration of their 90th anniversary July, 1988 at Temple Bethel. During the Friday evening and Saturday services six women spoke on the significance of the organization. Each member articulated the way in which participation in the group had enabled them to have a full and active church life. They demonstrated the bond that develops among CGSC women through the organization's activities.

Notes

[1] Manual of the Daughter's of Jerusalem and Sisters of Mercy — June 1898-June 1948 (Philadelphia: 1948), p. 21.

[2] *Manual of the Daughter's of Jerusalem* . . . , pp. 8–12.

[3] Beersheba Crowdy Walker, *The Life and Works of William Saunders Crowdy* (Philadelphia: Elfreth Walker, 1955), pp. 23, 25.

Conclusion

The project I have here undertaken opens up a considerable number of research opportunities for scholars interested in the role of religious movements in the process of black liberation in America. The history of the roles played by blacks in the development of the U.S. social structure is a field still in its infancy. Each additional piece of research contributes importantly to a comprehensive reconstruction of the arduous path from plantation slavery to the struggles of the present.

Traditional historical methods conveniently avoid carefully accounting for the role played by marginal elements of society. When history means narratives about great wars, and the great men who fought them, a great deal of significant information is excluded by definition. There have not been a lot of great black heroes, great black politicians, or great black thinkers discussed in traditionally conceived historical documents. It has not been until the civil rights outbursts of the fifties and sixties that this dimension of U.S. history has been seriously pursued.

This certainly has repercussions in the various fields of human studies. A much deeper problem, however, is central to my concerns and the purpose of this work. There are tremendous political and sociological ramifications that fall from the exclusion of important segments of U.S. history from history textbooks. Characterizations of the past shape the way we think about the present and act toward the future. By digging in to the various strongholds, be they oral or written, of the stories of marginalized participants in American history and disseminating the data found there, we are in fact shaping the consciousness of the people that represent our future.

The consequences of this study are considerably more than the successful completion of a piece of research. A piece of our past, previously muted by prejudice, has been revived. With each occurrence of such revival, we will have a deeper impression of the abilities and accomplishments of non-mainstream peoples. It is my hope that the research I have done will contribute to this important task.

Postscript

It has been more than five years since the writing of this honors thesis which has now taken on book form at the request of Garland publishing. Since this time I have had the privilege of many comments about this document, due to the fact that this is the first attempt of its kind. Frankly, I feel that a much more comprehensive history needs still to be written on each of the factions existing in the United States, South Africa and Jamaica. I have tried to include as comprehensive a bibliography as I was able to do with the resources at hand in Kansas and through interlibrary loan. It is my hope that someone may want to take it upon themselves to finish what I have offered as a brief sketch of this fascinating movement. I also was able to accumulate a substantial amount of archives given to me along the way which I will donate to Gordon Meltons overflowing library so that it will be available to whomever wants to carry the torch further. I would also suggest looking at my honor's thesis (which has been donated to various libraries across the country including the University of Kansas Library in Lawrence) in that you will find names of people whom were willing to communicate with me about their knowledge of the church.

Presently, I continue to be interested in the variety of religious expressions that coexist within North America. At this point in my life I am interested in how people exist daily due to the abject poverty and racism that many, especially African Americans and women, are subjected to. During my masters in social work at the University of Chicago, I was able to work in an economically distraught all black

community of west Chicago called Lawndale. From my
experiences as an intern there I was able to find my place of
full time employment in the housing projects of Cabrini
Green. In both places I have often been curious about how
people view themselves religiously and by what means they
seek out their religious expression. I am grateful to have had
the experience of being allowed to be a part of people's
lives, to be let in the door and asked to observe rituals,
family traditions, ways of communicating, confusion over
areas of abuse, ways of being which greatly vary from
house to house and community to community.

I have had the rare opportunity of meeting people who
remind me of the spirit of Crowdy, individuals whom I
believe have moved and will continue to thwart people into a
different realm of thinking. Whether it be the child who
intuitively says to her mother that although her treatment of
her daughter may not have always been well thought through
that it is durable due to the fact that much of her childhood
has yet to be lived out and her mother can travel with her
down the rest of the road of childhood having learned from
the past. Whether it be the husband who says that despite
having been subjected to loneliness, confusion and many
tears that it was an important reshaping and worth it now that
his hope and inspiration is beside him again. Whether it be
the many people I am privileged to work alongside at
Demicco Youth Services and to work with and learn from in
the form of clients, or if it be the academics that surround
our household daily who are writing sometimes many
articles and books at a time trying to preserve their thoughts
and the thoughts of others while passing it on to the students
they encounter daily, or if the people are the movers and
shakers of labour movements, artistic endeavors, business
structures, embracers of children and parenthood, supporters
and listeners of others despite age and wisdom . . . in
many I have encountered the charisma of people like
Crowdy lives on through them. It is amazing what many
people accomplish in a single day, the lives they are able to
impact without even realizing it. However, it is the people
who have come to the realization that their words and actions

are important, meaningful and powerful who are able to move people towards a different mode of expressing thought. We should all be encouraged to give worth to our thoughts by writing them down as Crowdy did, only then will we be less marginalized and more voices will be heard because we understand the necessity of ensuring that all minority groups need to preserve their innerworld so that generations of people can glean insight from the abilities and insights we have.

Appendix I

EVENING SERVICE FOR SABBATH

(Rabbi and Cantor open The Holy of Holies and Ark)

(Congregation stand)

Rabbi and Congregation: Blessed be the Lord who is blessed forever and ever.

(The Rabbi and Cantor go to their Podiums and remain standing)

SILENT MEDITATION

Blessed, praised, glorified, extolled, and exalted be the name of the Supreme King of Kings, the Holy One, blessed be He, who is the first and the last, and besides Him there is no God. Extol Him who is in the heavens — Lord is His name, and rejoice before Him. His Name is exalted above all blessing and praise. Amen.

Rabbi: Blessed be the Name of His glorious majesty forever and ever.

Rabbi and Congregation: Let the Name of the Lord be blessed henceforth and forever.

Anthem: ...."I Love Thy Church, O God"

Prayer

Song:..

Rabbi: Blessed art Thou, Lord our God, King of the Universe, who at Thy word bringest on the evenings. With wisdom, Thou openest the gates of heaven, and with understanding, Thou changest the times and causest the seasons to alternate. Thou arrangest the stars in their courses in the sky according to Thy will; Thou createst day and night, Thou rollest away light before darkness, and darkness before light, Thou causest the day to pass and the night to come, and makest the distinction between day and night – Lord of Hosts is Thy name. Eternal God, mayest Thou reign over us forever and ever. Blessed art Thou, O Lord, who bringest on the evenings.

Thou hast loved the House of Israel with everlasting love; Thou hast taught us the Torah, and precepts, laws and judgments. Therefore, Lord our God, when we lie down and when we rise up, we will speak of Thy laws, and rejoice in the words of Thy Torah and in Thy precepts forever more. Indeed, they are our life and the length of our days, we will meditate on them day and night. Mayest Thou never take away Thy love from us. Blessed art Thou, O Lord, who lovest Thy people, Israel.

(Congregation be seated)

Song:..

RESPONSIVE READING

Rabbi: True and trustworthy is all of this. We are certain that He is the Lord, our God, and no one else, and that we, Israel, are His people.

Congregation: It is He, our God, and no one else, and we, Israel, are His people.

Rabbi: It is He, our King, who redeemed us from the power of despots, delivered us from the grasp of all tyrants, avenged us of all our oppressors, and requited all our mortal enemies.

Congregation: He did great incomprehensible acts and countless wonders; He kept us alive, and did not let us slip.

Rabbi: He made us to tread upon the high places of our enemies, and upon Pharoah, with signs and wonders, He smote, in His wrath, all the first-born of Egypt, and brought His people, Israel, from their midst to enduring freedom.

Congregation: He made His children pass between the parts of the Red Sea, and engulfed their pursuers and their enemies in the depths.

Rabbi: His children beheld His might; they gave praise and thanks to His name, and willingly accepted His sovereignty.

Congregation: Moses and the children sang a song to Thee with great rejoicing. All of them said: Who is like Thee, O Lord, among the mighty? Who is like Thee, glorious in holiness, awe-inspiring in renown, doing wonders?

Rabbi: The children saw Thy majesty as Thou didst part the sea before Moses. This is my God! they shouted, and they said:

Congregation: The Lord shall reign forever and ever.

Rabbi: Through God's omnipotence, the heavens and earth were finished, and all their host. By the seventh day, God had completed all His work which He had made, and He rested on the seventh day from all His work in which He had been engaged. Then God blessed the seventh day and hallowed it, because on it He had rested from all His work which He had created.

Congregation: Blessed art Thou, Lord our God and God of our Fathers, God of Abraham, God of Isaac, and God of Jacob; great, mighty, and revered God, Supreme God, Master of heaven and earth.

Rabbi: He, with His word, was a shield to our fathers, and by His bidding, He will revive the dead. He is the Holy God, like whom there is none. He gives rest to His people on His holy Sabbath Day, for He is pleased to grant them rest. Him we will serve with reverence and awe, and to His name we will give thanks every day, constantly, in the fitting form of blessings. He is the God to whom thanks are due, the Lord of peace, who hallows the Sabbath and blesses the seventh day, who gives sanctified rest to a joyful people in remembrance of the creation.

Congregation: Our God and God of our fathers, be pleased with our rest. Sanctify us with Thy commandments and grant us a share in Thy Torah; satisfy us with Thy goodness and gladden us with Thy deliverance; purify our hearts to serve Thee in truth; and, In Thy gracious love, Lord our God, grant that we keep Thy holy Sabbath as a heritage and that Israel, who hallows Thy name, may rest on it. Blessed art Thou, O Lord, who hallowest the Sabbath.

Song: ....

SILENT PRAYER

(Congregation stand)

Be pleased, Lord our God, with Thy people Israel and with their prayer; restore the worship to Thy most holy sanctuary; accept Israel's offerings and prayer with gracious love. May the worship of Thy people, Israel, be ever pleasing unto Thee.

My God, guard my tongue from evil and my lips from speaking falsehood. May my soul be silent to those who insult me; be my soul lowly to all as the dust. Open my heart to Thy Torah, that my soul may follow Thy commands. Speedily defeat the counsel of all those who plan evil against me and upset their design. Do it for the glory of Thy name, do it for the sake of Thy power; do it for the sake of Thy holiness; do it for the sake of Thy Torah. That Thy beloved may be rescued, save with Thy right hand and answer me.

May the words of my mouth and the meditation of my heart be pleasing before Thee, O Lord, my Stronghold and my Redeemer. May He who creates peace in His high heavens create peace for us and for all Israel. Amen.

(Congregation be seated)

Song: .... "Hear My Prayer, O Lord"

(Cantor holds up cup of wine as Rabbi reads first sentence)

Rabbi: Blessed art Thou, Lord our God, King of the universe, who createst the fruit of the vine.

Blessed art Thou, Lord our God, King of the universe, who hast sanctified us with Thy commandments and has been pleased with us Thou hast graciously given us Thy holy Sabbath as a heritage, in remembrance of creation. The Sabbath is the first among the holy festivals which recalls the exodus from Egypt. Indeed Thou has graciously given us Thy holy Sabbath as a heritage. Blessed art Thou, O Lord, who hallowest the Sabbath.

Song: ...."Blessing and Glory"

MOURNERS' KADDISH
(Only if mourners are present)

(Mourners stand)

Mourners: Glorified and sanctified be God's great Name throughout the world which He has created according to His will. May He establish His Kingdom in your life-time and during your days, and within the life of the entire House of Israel, speedily and soon; and say. Amen.

Congregation: Amen.

Congregation: May His great Name be blessed forever and to all eternity.

Mourners: Blessed and praised, glorified and exalted, extolled and honored, adored and lauded be the Name of the Holy One blessed be He beyond all the blessings and hymns, praises and consolations that are ever spoken in the world; and say, Amen.

Congregation: Amen.

Mourners: May there be abundant peace from heaven, and life for us all and for all Israel; and say, Amen.

Congregation: Amen.

Mourners: He who creates peace in His celestial heights, may He create peace for us and for all Israel; and say, Amen.

Congregation: Amen.

(Mourners be seated)

Song:...

Rabbi: Grant, Lord our God, that we lie down in peace, and that we rise again, O our King, to life. Spread over us Thy shelter of peace, and direct us with good counsel of Thine own. Save us for Thy Name's sake; shield us, and remove from us every enemy and pestilence, sword and famine and grief remove the adversary from before us and from behind us shelter us in the shadow of Thy wings for Thou art our protecting and saving God; Thou art indeed a gracious and merciful God and King. Guard Thou our going out and coming in for life and peace, henceforth and forever. Do Thou spread over us Thy shelter of peace. Blessed art Thou, O Lord, who spreadest the shelter of peace over us and over all Thy people, Israel, Amen.

Song:...

Scripture

Song:...

(During song, Congregation stand. Rabbi and Cantor close Holy of Holies.)

Sermon

Song: ....

Preistly Benediction: .... Numbers 2:24–26

Appendix II

BLACK HISTORY QUESTIONS

1. Queen Ann Nzinga was the female Angolan leader who, in the mid 1600s successfully resisted, for 40 years, colonization by what European country?
   a) England   b) Portugal   c) France   d) Spain

2. Name the ancient Egyptian scholar and physician who has been called the "real father of medicine." He is acknowledged to have described the circulation of blood 4000 years before Europe discovered this important body function.
   a) King Tut   b) Ramses   c) Imhotep   d) Kush

3. Name the Santo Domingo revolutionary leader who led the only successful slave revolt in western history His defeat of Napoleon Bonaparte's expedition in 1803 led to the establishment of the independent state of Haiti, which has lasted to this day.
   a) Papa Doc   b) Maurice Bishop
   c) Toussaint L'Ouverture   d) Marcus Garvey

4. Haile Selassie was the nation's leader who repulsed the Italian invasion of his country in 1936. Claiming to be a direct descendant of King Solomon, he harshly ruled his poor E. African country, attempting to modernize and educate his largely illiterate people. Deposed and exiled, he died in 1975. What country did he rule?
   a) Egypt   b) Solalia   c) Ethiopia   d) Sudan

5. What is the name of the African Nation founded by Blacks of the American Colonization Society in 1822?

6. What is the name of the Black township, outside Johannesburg, S Africa, that experienced bloody rioting in 1976, growing out of Black student protests against the compulsory use of the Afrikaans language in the school?

7. What is the name of the archaeological site in Kenya, East Africa where, to date, the oldest human-like fossils have been found?
   a) Nairobi   b) Kikuyu   c) Mau Mau
   d) Olduvai Gorge

8.   Who was the Kenyan president and leader, nicknamed "The Old Man," who led his East African nation to freedom from British Colonialism?

9.   In 1889 Frederick Douglas was appointed U.S. Minister to this Caribbean nation. Name the country.

10.   Name the Black man who was the first to give his life in the skirmish later known as the Boston Massacre, which touched off the American Revolution. He rallied his comrades saying, "Do not be afraid," as he led the ranks. Today his name tops the list of the five carved in the monument erected to commemorate that historic night in Boston Commons.

11.   Jean Baptiste du Sable was the Black man who first established, in 1772, a small settlement, which later grew to become one of America's greatest cities. This establishment of this midwest juncture opened new doors to the West and North. Name the city.

12.   Which one of the 13 original New England colonies was the first to legalize slavery?

13.   What Pennsylvania-based religious group was the first to sign an anti-slavery resolution in 1688, which became the first formal protest against slavery in the Western Hemisphere?

14.   Who was the man who organized the first Black Masonic Lodge in America, in Philadelphia in 1787?

SLAVERY/ABOLITION

15.   What is the name of the Virginia settlement at which the arrival of 20 Black indentured servant, in 1619, ushered in the beginning of the Atlantic Slave Trade?

16.   The white abolitionist, John Brown, played one of the many key roles in the drama that led to the Civil War. His raid on a federal arsenal in Virginia in 1859, has become famous in American history. Name the place in Virginia where this arsenal was located.

17.   What is the title of the novel written by Harriet Beecher Stowe, which appeared in 1852? This novel sold over 300,000 copies in one year and won over countless thousand of sympathizers to the abolitionist cause.

18.   Called The Black Prophet by some, this visionary slave revolutionary led a small band of slaves on a two-day insurrection that rocked the area of Southampton, Virginia in August of 1831. He fled to the nearby Dismal Swamp where he remained at large for six weeks before being captured.

19.   Freedom's Journal was the first Black newspaper to be published in the U.S. in 1872. In what city?
       a) New York   b) Philadelphia   c) Boston   d) Chicago

20.   Name the free Black man who published and distributed the militant anti-slavery pamphlet, Appeal to the Colored People of World, in 1829, which caused a furor among slaveholders throughout the country.

21.   What is the name of the slave ship, on which the African leader Joseph Cinque and his followers revolted against their captors and eventually won their freedom and returned to Africa?

22.   What is the name of the famous Supreme Court Decision that, in 1857, opened federal territory to slavery, denied citizenship rights to Blacks and decreed that slaves do not become free when taken into free territory? It was named after that slave who sued his master for his freedom.

23.   What is the name of the Florida Indian nation that offered refuge to fugitive slaves, intermarried with them and fought along with them against the U.S. government in a series of wars in the mid 1800s?

24.   What was the title of Frederick Douglass' abolitionist newspaper which he first published in New York in 1847?

25.   P.B.S. Pinchback was born a slave in Mississippi, and this Black politician eventually made his home in another southern state. During Reconstruction he became a state senator, School Board Director of a major city's school

system, senator, lieutenant governor and in 1872, governor of the state. What state claimed this first Black governor?

26.   In 1863, President Abraham Lincoln issued an important document, that declared that all slaves in rebellious areas be free. What was this document called?

27.   In 1865 in Tennessee this terrorist group was formed by whites with the expressed purpose of reasserting white supremacy and minimizing the influence of the Union in the South. Name the group.

28.   In 1881 in Tennessee a series of railroad laws were enacted which set a trend for many other states throughout the South. These laws legalized segregation in many public facilities and services. The laws were named after a popular character in a minstrel song.

29.   This post Civil War Act of Congress in 1867, ratified the 14th Amendment and guaranteed Blacks the right to vote, giving Blacks the majority voice in most southern states.

POLITICS/MASS MOVEMENT

30.   In 1912, Marcus Garvey founded an organization that grew to become one of the largest and most influential organizations in the Black world. At its height, this organization claimed four million dues paying members, a daily newspaper, a shipping line and many other impressive enterprises. Name the organization.

31.   Even though Garvey's UNIA was highly urbanized, its stronghold was the Southern United States, the most thoroughly organized Garveyite area in the world. With 74 branches, name the southern state that was the leading center of the UNIA.

32.   During the 1930s, this religious leader drew items of thousands of followers. His Peace Mission Movement provided free meals and shelter throughout the Depression Era. At the height of his power, his movement operated 25 restaurants, two groceries, several barber shops and a fleet of

vegetable, fish, fruit and coal wagons. The true believers called him God.

33. This politician was the son of an eminent Harlem minister who pastored the largest Black congregation in America. First elected to the House of Representatives in 1944, he offset his reputation for absenteeism by pushing civil rights and other legislation favorable to Blacks through Congress.

34. In 1967, Carl Stokes became the first Black mayor of a major American city. Name the city.

35. What is the name of the Black security guard who detected and detained a group of men installing surveillance equipment in the Democratic Party National Headquarters at the Watergate office complex in Washington, DC, that led to the infamous Watergate Scandal and rocked the Nixon administration?

36. What is the name of the former congresswoman from New York who was the first Black woman to sit in the U.S. House of Representatives, in 1969?

37. Who was the first Black appointed as an Associate Justice of the Supreme Court in 1967, by President Johnson?

38. In May 1966, this prominent Black activist spokesman was named as the head of the Student Non-Violent Coordinating Committee (SNCC), charting a new course for the "Black Power" doctrine. Name him.

39. In 1966, Huey Newton and Bobby Seale founded, Oakland, CA, an organization which proposed a 10-pointed program which included reparations for past abuses of Blacks, release of Black prisoners and trial of Blacks by Black juries. What was the name of this organization?

40. On what date was Dr. Martin Luther King Jr. assassinated in Memphis, TN?

41. What was the controversial statement made by Malcolm X in 1963 concerning the Kennedy assassination that caused

Malcolm's suspension from the Nation of Islam by Elijah Muhammad?

42. In his later years, he was called "Mr. Civil Rights." He served the NAACP in many capacities, including executive director, for over 50 years. This former editor of the NAACP's Crisis Magazine, was awarded the "Medal of Freedom" by President Johnson in 1969.

43. In 1905, in New York, 129 Black intellectuals from 14 states met and organized the Niagara Movement which became the forerunner of this important civil rights organization, which still exists today.

44. In 1954, this unanimous landmark Supreme Court decision overturned the "separate but equal" doctrine that since 1896 legitimized segregation in the schools and other public facilities. Name this landmark case.

45. In 1955, in Montgomery, AL, this brave Black woman refused to surrender her seat on a bus to a white man and was arrested. Dr. Martin Luther King called for a Black bus boycott which sparked the Civil Rights Movement. Name this important Black Heroine.

46. In 1963, this prominent civil rights leader was assassinated in the doorway of his home in Jackson, MS.

47. In 1964, in New York City, Malcolm X resigned from the Black Muslim Movement to form a new organization. What was the name of that new organization?

48. For six days in August, 1965, looting, burning and rioting plunged this predominantly Black section of Los Angeles into a state of anarchy, which resulted from the mistreatment of a Black youth by a white policeman. Name this section of Los Angeles.

49. In 1926, this important and influential civil rights and labor leader founded the Brotherhood of Sleeping Car Porters.

50. Pamela Johnson is the Black woman who, in 1981, was named to a position on the *Ithaca Journal*, becoming the first

Black woman to hold such a position with a major newspaper in the U.S. What position does she hold?

51.   Who was the woman called "Black Moses," a major conductor on the Underground Railroad, who returned to the South 19 times leading over 300 slaves to freedom in the North and Canada?

52.   This self-proclaimed "Pilgrim of God" was the first woman orator to speak out against slavery. Having set upon a personal journey for truth and freedom, she became one of the most popular speakers for Black and women's rights. She coined the popular rallying cry for women's rights — "Ain't I a woman."

53.   Name the women who, in 1905, invented a hair softener, grower and straightening comb, that revolutionized the cosmetics industry in the Black community. Her ingenuity and ability helped her to become the first Black, self-made millionaire in America.

54.   Purchased from the slave-auction block at the age of eight, this little girl mastered the English language within 16 weeks. By 1773 she was an internationally known and published poet. She traveled to London, was hailed as a prodigy, and upon her return was issued a personal invitation to visit George Washington.

55.   This outstanding Black woman rose from a field hand picking cotton to the position of confidante and advisor to Franklin Roosevelt. The 17th child of sharecropping parent, this outstanding educator founded and built a well-known southern liberal-arts college that bears her name.

SCIENCE AND TECHNOLOGY

56.   Dr. Percy Julian was the renowned Black chemist who, in 1935, developed a drug for the treatment of what dreaded eye disease?
a) retinitus   b) astigmatism   c) color blindness   d) glaucoma

57. Name the Black inventor whose automatic lubrication system, devised in 1872, allowed for the continuous flow of oil to machinery without the necessity of stopping the machines. This Black man held over 50 patents and it is from him that the expression "The Real McCoy" originated.

58. Who was the free-born inventor, mathematician, astronomer and essayist, called the "sable genius"? He made, completely of wood, the first clock wholly made in America. This clock kept accurate time for over 20 years. He is best known for taking part in laying out the plans for the City of Washington, D.C.

59. Name the famous agricultural-chemist whose crop research at the Tuskegee Institute led to better and more productive farming in the South. He also discovered a multitude of products and uses for the soybean, peanut and sweet potato.

60. This Black physician and scientist was the pioneer in Blood Plasma Research. His method of storing blood plasma for the injured and wounded was a significant fact in turning the tide in the allied war effort in World War II. Ironically, this Black man died from loss of blood, sustained in an auto accident, having been denied admission to a "white" hospital.

61. Jan Matzeliger was the Black inventory who revolutionized this industry in 1863 with his patented invention of a "lasting" machine which made production of these items easier and faster. He worked 10 years on his invention, which all the industry experts claimed was impossible to make. What manufactured items did Matzeliger improve the production of?

62. This Arctic explorer, for years lost in the shadows of Admiral Peary, was in actuality the first man to discover the North Pole. Favored by the Eskimos because of hi dark complexion, this explorer proved indispensable on Peary's many expeditions. Name the explorer who actually placed the flag on the North Pole.

63. Daniel Hale Williams was an Outstanding physician and surgeon. In Chicago, in 1893, he accomplished an important

surgical procedure that had not been done before. What operation did he perform?

64. This Black inventory was granted a patent for the first incandescent lamp with carbon filament. This man also made the drawings for Alexander Graham Bell's telephone and became the chief draftsman for General Electric and Westinghouse.

65. Who was the Black woman playwright, whose play, *A Raisin In the Sun*, won the New York Drama Critics Circle Award in 1959? She was the first Black to win this award.

66. Who was the outstanding historian who founded the Association for the Study of Negro Life and History in 1915, which was later named the Association for the Study of Afro-American Life and History. He is responsible for founding Black History Month. One of his most famous works is The Miseducation of the Negro.

67. In 1940, this important Black educator and founder of Tuskegee Institute became the first Black to be honored on a U.S. postage stamp. Valued at 10 cents, the stamp belonged to the "Famous American Series." Who was he?

68. During the decade after World War I, an exciting cultural movement emerged in the Black community. Characterized by a spirit of protest and pride and reflected in a resurgence of Black literature, art, music and politics. Named after a well-known New York community, what was this cultural phenomenon called?

69. This prolific poet, novelist, essayist and world traveler flourished during the Harlem Renaissance. One of the most famous poem "The Negro Speaks of Rivers" inspired the theme of the Afro-American Pavilion at the 1984 World's Fair. Who was he?

70. This novelist, poet, NAACP official and diplomat is most famous for his poem, "Lift Every Voice and Sing," which, when set to music by his brother, became "The Black National Anthem." One of his most famous written works is The Autobiography of an Ex Colored Man.

71. This Harlem Renaissance writer is perhaps best known for the poem "If We Must Die," in which he admonishes Black people to fight and die with dignity. The book *Harlem Shadows* made his reputation as a poet, and the novels *Home To Harlem, Banjo* and *Banana Bottom* insured his place among great Black writers.

72. What is the name of the first Black university founded in the U.S. in Pennsylvania in 1853? It was originally named the Ashmum Institute.

73. In 1894, in Cambridge, MA, this important Black scholar, writer and philosopher became the first Black man to receive a Ph.D. from Harvard University.

74. Name the Black poetess, who, in 1950, became the first Black to win a Pulitzer Prize for poetry.

75. Who as the internationally known Black photographer whose photographs of Harlem and its people created a half-century long visual history of the area? His 1969 exhibition "Harlem On My Mind" at the New York Metropolitan Museum of Art, brought him international recognition.

SPORTS/ENTERTAINMENT

76. Jesse Owens won four gold medals in the Olympics, a standard of athletic greatness which inspired Carl Lewis in his 4-gold-medal achievement in 1984 in Los Angeles. Name the year and the city in which Jesse Owens accomplished his feat.

77. Who was the legendary Black cowboy, who was given the title "Deadwood Dick" for his bronco-busting, calf-roping and riding techniques displayed at Deadwood, S. Dakota in 1876.
    a) Nat Love   b) Bill Pickett   c) James Beckworth
    d) Sam Jones

78. Who was the New Orleans born gospel singer who became known a the "Queen of Gospel Music"? Her 1945 hit "Move Up A Little Higher" sold over a million copies.

79.   Who was the controversial saxophonist whose revolutionary "sheets of sound" technique influenced an entire school of avant-garde jazz musicians? He played with such greats as Dizzy Gillespie, Miles Davis and Theolonious Monk. He died in 1967.

80.   Who was the outstanding jazz composer and orchestra leader who is considered to have made the most pervasive contribution to the development of jazz in the United States? His classics, such as "Mood Indigo" and "Take The A Train," are still being enjoyed today. The recent Broadway musical "Sophisticated Ladies" was done in his honor.

81.   In 1919, Fritz Pollard became the first Black to play professional football for a major team, the Akron Indians. In 1916 Pollard had been the first Black to play in a prestigious college bowl game for Brown University. What Bowl did he play in?

82.   Who was the first Black man to coach a major professional sports team and what team did he coach?

83.   Rising from a brutalizing background, this singer became the leading jazz vocalist of the 1940s. Some of her big hits included "Lover Man" and "Gloomy Sunday." At one time or another virtually every major musician of the day appeared with her during her career. She was known as "Lady Day."

84.   Name the multi-talented artist, athlete, singer, actor who in 1949, shocked the government by speaking out against the Black American war effort on behalf of a racist society. His role a Othello on Broadway in 1943 ran for 296 performances, and was highly praised by the New York drama critics.

85.   Hattie McDaniel played a role in this classic film that earned her the first Black Academy Award. What was the name of that film?

Reprinted from *The Black Collegian*

Appendix III

ON BECOMING A MEMBER OF THIS RELIGIOUS ORGANIZATION

1.   When three chairs are set out, the candidate takes a seat.

2.   He is asked to declare why he made the choice. Romans 10:9–10 (See Section 9 of Church Constitution Rev. 1959, pp. 15–16.)

3.   He is scheduled for Immersion (Baptism) and whole Armour. St. John 1:21–23, St. Matthem 26:26–27, St. John 13:1–8, St Matthew 6:9–14, St. John 20:22, Exodus 20:1–18.

4.   He is asked to be in attendance at Sabbath Services which begin on Friday evening and end Saturday evening. Exodus 20:8–11.

5.   He is to wear the uniform prescribed by the Prophet — God's Messenger — so as to place everyone on equality in the Kingdom of God, and to teach Biblical Truths and Lessons.

6.   He is to observe all High Days which include:
     a. The Sabbath Day
     b. Rosh Hashannah
     c. Yom Kippur
     d. Re-establishment Day
     e. Feast of the Tenth Month
     f. Passover
     g. Shavouth
     h. Purim

7.   pray three times a day, evening, morning, and noon. Daniel 6:10 (12th Hour, a.m.; 6th Hour, noon; 12th Hour, evening).

8.   Every morning take three swallows of water before prayer for health's sake. (Prophet Wm. S. Crowdy).

9.   Observe the Ten Commandments. Exodus 20:1–18.

10. Engage in religious practices — Micah 6:8, 2nd Timothy Chapter 6, Micah 3:7–17.

11. Join the affiliated auxiliaries or departments in order to adequately work in God's vineyard: (choir, Daughter's Auxiliary, Sons of Abraham, M.&W.D.A., Y.P.I.L., Sabbath School, Deacons, ushers, etc.)

    A. Daughters of Jerusalem and Sisters of Mercy

       This organization has the following responsibilities:

       1. Look after the sick and indigent.

       2. Prepare new candidates for various ceremonies when entering the fold.

       3. Take care of the Pastor's food, clothing, and pulpit.

       4. Take care of visiting ministers and members.

       5. Take care of the beautification of the Tabernacle.

       6. Comfort the bereaved.

       7. Look out for widows and orphans.

    B. Sabbath School: This organization teaches the members about religious doctrine and about our duties toward God and man.

    C. The Choir: This organization supplies the music for the Tabernacle; sings God's praises.

    D. The Sons of Abraham: A men's group that sees that the Temple is comfortable and fitting for worship.

    E. Y.P.I.L.: A youth group that serves the Tabernacle. It teaches manners, group participation, and religious protocol.

    F. M.&W.D.A.: An adult group that services the Tabernacle by fostering literary programs and finances for cultural development.

Appendix IV

"ISRAEL SHALL BE SAVED IN THE LORD

PROGRAM

✡

Sunday Evening, March 30, 1980 — 6:00 O'clock

TEMPLE ANTHEM,	"I love Thy Church, O God"
INVOCATION	
SELECTION	Union Choir
WELCOME ADDRESS	Elder Andrew Love
SELECTION	Union Choir
SCRIPTURE — Exodus 12:1–14	Elder Phillip McNeil
SELECTION	Union Choir
SERMON	Rabbi Levi S. Plummer

SEDER

HOST   Rabbi Levi S. Plummer

First Day — Monday, March 31, 1980 — 10:00 A.M.

DEVOTIONAL SERVICE   Evangelist Judah A. Person

7:00 P.M.

MEN AND WOMEN'S RALLY

Second Day — Tuesday, April 1, 1980 — 10:00 A.M.

DEVOTIONAL SERVICE   Evangelist J. David Morrison

10:30 A.M.

MUSIC DEPARTMENT
Elder Charles D. Plummer, Grand Choirmaster
Elder Thomas E. Stephenson, Grand Cantor

Third Day — Wednesday, April 2, 1980 — 10:00 A.M.

DEVOTIONAL SERVICE   Evangelist Clifton C. Farrar

10:30 A.M.

DAUGHTER'S AUXILIARY
Sister L. Bernice Plummer, C.M.S. Presiding

Fourth Day — Thursday, April 3, 1980 — 10:00 A.M.

DEVOTIONAL
SERVICE   Evangelist Benjamin J. Quatltebaum

10:30 A.M.

RELIGIOUS EDUCATION DEPARTMENT
Elder John H. Eaves, General Superintendent
Elder Phillip McNeil, Assistant General Superintendent

WITH AN EVERLASTING SALVATION"

"BUT THOU, ISRAEL, ART MY SERVANT,

PROGRAM

✡

Fifth Day — Friday, April 4, 1980 — 10:00 A.M.
DEVOTIONAL SERVICE   Evangelist Moses Farrar

10:30 A.M.
NATIONAL M.&W.D.A.
NATIONAL Y.P.I.L.

Beginning of Sabbath Service — 6:00 P.M.
TEMPLE ANTHEM,   "I Love Thy Church, O God"
INVOCATION
WORSHIP SERVICE   Elder Robert Madison
SERMON   Evangelist-at-Large A.M. Williamson

Sabbath Day (Saturday), April 5, 1980 — 9:00 A.M.
TEMPLE ANTHEM,   "I Love Thy Church O God"
INVOCATION
SABBATH   Elder John H. Eaves, Gen'l Supt.
SCHOOL   Elder Phillip McNeil, Asst. Gen'l Supt.
WORSHIP SERVICE
SERMON   Rabbi Levi S. Plummer

AFTERNOON SESSION
MUSICAL SELECTIONS

Sixth Day — Sunday, April 6, 1980 — 10:00 A.M.
DEVOTIONAL   Evangelist.-at-Large, Jehu O. Smith
SERVICE

TEMPLE BUILDING FUND

Seventh Day — Monday, April 7, 1980 — 9:00 A.M.
DEVOTIONAL   Evang.-at-Large Joseph H. Stephenson
SERVICE
REMARKS   Rabbinical council

AFTERNOON SESSION
ORDINATIONS — APPOINTMENTS — AWARDS
ANNOUNCEMENTS
CLOSING ADDRESS   Rabbi L.S. Plummer

JACOB WHOM I HAVE CHOSEN."

Bibliography

Primary Sources

NOTE: Primary Sources in this section are located at the Topeka State Historical Society in Topeka, Kansas. The sources were donated by Beersheba Granison, grand-daughter of the founder.

JOSELRAMA, Bishop J.A. Crowdy. This is a tabernacle bulletin.

Church of God and Saints of Christ Directory — In Honor of our 50th Anniversary — 1896–1946 —, Dedicated to Bishop H.Z. Plummer, 420 pp. Contains pictures and histories of various churches.

Church of God and Saints of Christ Minutes, 1917. 23 pp. Contains a brief biography of Prophet Crowdy, a picture of Cardinal Bishop H.Z. Plummer and the Presbytery Board, the Stone of Truth, history of the church, and an official program of Founders Day Ceremony held in Varick Memorial Church at 19th and Catherine in Philadelphia, PA., Nov. 7–10, 1940.

Church of God and Saints of Christ Minutes, 1917. Fragment consisting of pp. 1–32 and 59–72. It has pictures of Bishop J.W. Crowdy, Bishop Wm. H. Plummer, Elder Calvin Skinner, St. Martha Bank (Grandmother Sarah), and it contained the minutes of 1917.

Church of God and Saints of Christ Song Book. Compiled by Elder W.J. Plummer: Grand Choir Master, "Sweet Songs of Zion." 74 pp. Contains pictures of Prophet Crowdy and St. Anne Frame (Chief Choirmistress).

I love thy church of God. pp. 11–126. This is a song book.

Let no man take thy crown. 74 pp. This is a song book.

Crowdy, William S. *The Bible Story Revealed.* Belleville, VA: Church of God and Saints of Christ Publishing House, December 16, 1902.

Funeral Services for Joseph Russell Cordery, Jr. — June 26, 1967– Aug. 25, 1986. 3 pp. Gives a brief biography of this church member and displays the church's funeral format.

Manual of the Daughters of Jerusaleum and Sisters of Mercy, June 1898–June 1948. (Philadelphia, 1948), 43 pp. It talks about the first officers, Grandmother Sarah, Father Abraham, Grand Rachel, Grandfather Abraham, Grand Leah, Assistant Grand Rachel, Grand Mary, Grand Storehouse Mistress, Mother Exhorter — and functions thereof. Passovers, Assemblies, delegates, established local auxilaries, tabernacle numbers, daughters table, membership office, committees, ceremony for installation, by-laws, rituals, blessing of church and infants, footwashing ceremony, mourning, children's programs, and daughter's songs.

Souvenir Journal Service of Dedication — Temple Beth El — (Suffolk, Virginia), 100 pp. The church is located at 3927 Bridge Rd. Rabbi Levi Solomon Plummer is president. Contains congratulations from various pictures of people from other temples.

Souvenir Program — Installation Service for Bishop Lewis S. Plummer at the Church of God and Saints of Christ, 68 Pond St., (Providence, Rhode Island), 13 pp. Contains a page of background on Bishop Plummer. It also has ads from members who own businesses and greetings from other churches.

The Constitution Laws and Minutes. 29 pp. These are the first minutes taken of the church on Oct. 10, 1899 in Lawrence, KS. Contains the minutes of the General Assn. of Daughters of Jerusaleum and Sisters of Mercy in Lawrence, on Oct. 12, 1899.

The Constitution and Minutes from 1901–1903 of the Church of God and Saints of Christ for the second and third district assembly of the Eastern District. 147 pp. (Philadelphia, Pennsylvania: Church of God and Saints of Christ Publishing House, 1420 Fitzwater St). 70 pp. The constitution and minutes from 1904–1907 are also included in the same bound edition (77 pp.).

The Constitution Laws and Minutes. Reports from 1907–1913 of The Church of God and Saints of Christ. Cambridge, Mass.: Junius S. Mobley, 88 pp.

The Daughters Newsletter. (Published by Daughters of Jerusaleum and Sisters of Mercy, Vol. 23, August, 1969), No. 2., 3 pp. Discusses sermons, graduations, weddings, and obituaries.

The Seven Keys. Seven rules/guidelines to follow when one is a member of the church. Promulgated by Crowdy as a basic theological and ethical document.

The Weekly Prophet. Vol. 2, No. 17, (Portsmouth,Va., November 10, 1950). The cost was 7 cents. This issue is 4 pp. in length, and talks about "Spiritual Osmosis," "Human Weakness," "Belleville Report," "Our Jeanette Keeling Honored at Annual Fish Bowl Classic," "Discussion of Race Relations conducted by Richmond Pastor," "Three

Tabernacles have united service." The Weekly Prophet is issued every Friday at Portsmouth,VA.

The Weekly Prophet. Official Organ of the Church of God and Saints of Christ, Issue #1013, July 18, 1986. Tells of the 86th Annual Passover Memorial in Belleville, Va.

Walker, Beersheba Crowdy. *The Life and Works of William Saunders Crowdy.* (Philadelphia: Elfreth Walker, 1955), 62 pp. This is the last hardcover copy of the first edition. It gives a detailed account of the founder.

Walker, E.J.P. *The Armour Bearer* — Bishop J.M. Groves as I knew him — An Interview. (Philadelphia: E. Walker, 1961), 12 pp. Contains pictures of Prophet Crowdy, Howard Plummer, Bishop M. Groves, Elder Sydney and the author. One interesting note is that it mentions the factions of the COGSOC which occured in 1908.

NOTE:Primary sources in this section were found in a Personal Library of an Archivist of Black Religious Movements

A Brief History of the Department of Sabbath School — 1976, 27 pp. This was done by Howard Z. and Levi S. Plummer in Belleville, Va.

Basic Tabernacle Instructions. 12 pp.

Ceremonies for Sabbath High Holy Days and Festivals, 60 pp. This document was printed in 1984 for the members of the church. It has the order of worship for various ceremonies.

Constitution of the Church of God and Saints of Christ for the Grand Assembly of the U.S., 30 pp. A 1949 revision of the constitution made in Lawrence.

Crowdy, William S. *The Bible Gospel Told: The Revelation of God Revealed.* (Washington: Church of God and Saints of Christ, 1902).

Customs and Practices with Biblical References, 6 pp.

Duties and Responsibilities of Sabbath School Officers, April 6, 1980, 23 pp.

Eightieth Annual Feast of Passover — 5740 (1980) — , 20 pp. Contains mainly pictures.

History of the Daughters of Jerusalem and Sisters of Mercy, 23 pp. Lecture given by St. Barbar O. Dickerson, Jr. Grand Rachel, at the 1964 and 1965 Daughters' Regional Meetings.

New Year's Greetings, 1936, 4 pp. A message from the leader in 1936, namely Bishop H.Z. Plummer, G.F.A.

Passover, 7 pp. On do's and don'ts during.

Praying Positions, 3 pp. Distributed by Levi S. Plummer on November 12, 1987.

Prophet William S. Crowdy's Great Prophetic Sermons — 1903, 35 pp. of documentation on various sermons that Crowdy gave over his years as head of the church.

Sabbath School Annual of the Department of Religious Education, 76 pp. Compiled by L.S. Plummer and Andrew R. Love in April of 1986.

Souvenir Jounal Service of Dedication — *Phase 2* — . This was put out in April 11, 1987. It is a lengthy document containing mainly pictures and words of thanks from various members.

Temple Beth El — *Department of Home and Foreign Missions*, 11 pp. A missionary packet put out by Rabbi L.S. Plummer.

The Pastor's table committee and the pastor's clothing committee. This is a document from 1974 describing the work of the two named committees.

The Weekly Prophet. I have over 30 different issues from the period 1978–1988. I also have one copy from 1939 and a 1973 directory of churches.

Secondary Sources

Ahlstrom, Sydney. *Theology in America: The Major Protestant Voices from Puritanism to Neo-Orthodoxy.* (New York: Bobbs-Merrill Co. Inc., 1967).

Anderson, Marion. *My Lord, What a Morning.* (New York:Viking, 1956), p.16. Tells of the author's (the author is a famous black singer) grandfather, who was a black jew. This was a reference from Landing and gives no clear reference to the church.

Bennet, Lerone. *Before the Mayflower* — *A History of Black America.* (Chicago: Johnson Publishing Co., 1982).

Berger, Graneum. *Black Jews in America*. (New York: Federation of Jewish Philanthropies of N.Y.,1978), pp. 68–69, 205. Talks about the church under the chapter "Synagogue or Cult." Notes that Crowdy's church is a forerunner of Black Jewish cults. Crowdy asserted that Black Americans were in reality the Hebrews of the Bible and that he was destined to restore them to their rightful place as members of Israel.

"Bishop Howard Plummer heard by Mass. NAACP: Belleville leader shares program with Elite." *Norfolk Journal and Guide*, May 25, 1935. Sernett, p. 395.

Blackmar, Frank W. *Kansas: A Cyclopedia of State History*. (Chicago: Standard, 1912), pp. 345–346. Gives a typical two paragraph synopsis of the church. At the time of writing he cited three Kansas organizations with a membership of 78.

Blassingame, John W. *The Slave Community*. (New York: Oxford University Press, 1972).

Brotz, Howard M. *The Black Jews of Harlem*. (New York: Schocken Books 1970), p. 9. Tells of Prophet Crowdy's successor Bishop William H. Plummer who personified himself as Grand Father Abraham. He was a dictator who takes possession of all property of his adherents and doles out to them whatever he wishes.

Brotz, Howard M. "Negro Jews in the U.S.," *Phylon*, 13, 1952, pp. 324–337.

Brown, Jesse Edward. "Doctrinal Synopsis of the Church of God and Saints of Christ" (Rochester: Colgate Rochester Divinity School, 1981), 21 pp. This was a term paper distributed to the elders of the CGSOC.

____. "Prophet William Saunders Crowdy and the Church of God and Saints of Christ: The Implications of his life and thought for the mission of the church." (Rochester: Colgate Rochester Divinity School, 1986), 264 pp. Offers a member perspective insight about the church.

Business and Resident Directory of Guthrie and Logan Coutny for the Year Commencing Sept 1, 1892. (Guthrie, Oklahoma: Frankie G. Poutry Publishers, 1892). Gives the address of W.S. Crowdy.

Chambers, Mary Anne. "Black Residential Segregation in Lawrence, Kansas, 1876–1919." This was done in 1970 by a student for Prof. Katzman. It is helpful and gives a good Lawrence map.

Clark, Elmer Talmage. *The Small Sects in America*. (Nashville: Cokesbury Press, 1937), p. 188f. Says that Crowdy said that the ten lost tribes of Israel are the progenitors of the American blacks.

Clark, Elmer Talmage. *Small Sects in America*. Revised edition, (New York: Abingdon, 1947), pp.151–153, 225. Tells of the church in detail based on the *1936 Census of Religious Bodies*.

Clifton, Johnson. *God Struck me Dead*. (Nashville: Fisk University Press, 1969). This book was recommended to me by Preston Mangana, who said he often suggests this to people inquiring about the faith. Gives various accounts of black persons personal religious experiences.

Coleman, Robert T. *American Examiner — Jewish Week*, Nov. 16, 1974, p. 35. Describes how some Jewish communities wanted to convince Howard Z. Plummer (recently deceased spiritual leader) to discard Christological teachings and become more traditionally Jewish.

Crawford, George W. *Prince Hall and His Followers: Being a Monograph on the Legitimacy of Negro Masonry*. (New York: AMS Press Inc., 1971). Gives an autobiographical description of Prince Hall and the Negro Masons he established in 1784, of which W.S. Crowdy was a member.

Daily Dispatch (East London Paper) — June 8 1920 and Dec 2 1921. Gives an account of the South African church.

Dary, David. *Lawrence-Douglas County, Kansas. An Informal History*. (Lawrence: Allen Press, 1982), p. 194. States that the Unitarian church was established in October 8, 1855 and that the first black church was the African Methodist Episcopal in 1862.

Dobrin, Arthur. "A History of the Negro Jews in America." (Unpublished paper City College of the City University of New York 1965, Schamburg Collection, New York City Public Library). In Appendix 1 p. 47 he erroneously refers to Crowdy as Crouder and later Cherry. This might explain why the *Encyclopedia of American Religion* cited Fauset because Fauset talks of Cherry.

Driscoll, Charles B. "Major Prophets in Kansas." *American Mercury*, May 1926, pp. 18–26. As J.E. Landing pointed out in his bibliographic information, this source shows that this was not only a black or unique phenomenan.

Eddy, Norman G. "Store Front Religion." *Religion in Life*, Vol. 28, Winter, 1958–1959, pp. 68–85. I found this in Salisbury. Eddy talks about the church on pp. 78–83.

Edgar, Robert Russell. *The Fifth Seal: Enoch Mgijima, the Israelites and the Bulhoek Massacre, 1921.* (Los Angeles: University of California Press, 1977), pp.17–52. Gives insight into the church in Africa and its history.

Emporia Daily Republican, June 24, 1898. Gives an account of the first general assembly of the church held in Emporia, KS.

Emporia Gazette, Nov. 3, 1949. "Mrs. Ellen Burton is member of Emporia's First Colored Family." This is a seven column newspaper clipping which describes Mrs. Burton's life and her descendants. I found her name in Manual of Daughters of Jerusalem. I had no luck contacting descendants.

Fishel, Leslie H. jr. & Quarles, Benjamin. *The Black American: A Documentary History.* (New York: William Morrow, 1970).

Gerber, Israel J. *The Heritage Seekers.* (Middle Village: Jonathon David Publishers, 1977), p. 69. Tells of the fact that blacks were attempting to establish an acceptable racial identity (complete with culture and history) and thus churches like Crowdy's were established.

Goodnight, Lizzy E. "Negroes of Lawrence." (Master's Thesis, Kansas University, 1903). Zavelo mentions this thesis as a source but I failed to see a mention of the church.

Gordon, Jacob U. *The Black Church in Kansas: A guide to the black community.* (Lawrence: University of Kansas, 1985). He has a helpful bibliograpy.

Grimshaw, W.H. *Official History of Freemasonry: Among the Colored People in North America.* (New York: Broadway Publishing Company, 1969). Gives the history of Freemasonry in Guthrie, Oklahoma — the place where Crowdy resided much of his adult life.

Gruver, Rebecca B. *An American History.* Volume 1 and 2. (Reading: Addison-Wesley Pub. Co., 1978).

Hopfe, Lewis M. *Religions of the World.* (Encino, California: Glenco Publishing, 1979). This was useful for religious data.

Horowitz, Frances D. "A Jewish Woman in Academic America," *Seeing Female: Social Roles and Personal Lives.* (New York:Greenwood Press), pp. 53–65.

Jacobs, Steven and Windsor, Rudolph. *The Hebrew Heritage of Our West African Ancestors.* (Wilmington: Rose Lee, 1971). Shows a picture of Temple Beth El in Virginia and talks a little of the church.

Jones, Raymond Julias. *A comparative study of religious cult behavior among Negroes.* (Washington D.C.: The Graduate School of Howard University 1939), pp. 4, 20, 60, 100–104, 125. Gives a lengthy description of a church service in 1939.

Kansas City Star, March 27, 1909. "Strange Sect of Negroes — Lawrence, KS the home of an extraordinary faith." This article is the only material I have that gives a detailed account of a worship service.

Landes, Ruth. "Negro Jews in Harlem." *Jewish Journal of Sociology*, No. 9, December 1967, pp.175–189. Tells of her 1933 study of the "Negro Jews in Harlem."

Landis, Benson. *Yearbook Of American Churches.* (Philadelphia: Sower Printing Co., 1943), p. 22. Tells of the origin of the church and the name of the founder, the doctrine, statistics, and the name of a bishop.

____. 1945 Edition, p. 21.

____. 1947 Edition, p. 21. Same as the 1943 Edition but excludes the statistics.

____. 1949 Edition, p. 22. Same as the 1947 Edition but includes new statistics.

____. 1952 Edition, pp. 29–30. Tells of the churches in the British West Indies, Africa, and the U.S.A., includes more detail of the doctrine, some new statistics on sabbath schools, and lists an elder.

____. 1962 Edition, p. 36. Gives more detail on the general organization of the church, includes a list of eight officers, provides a list of other organizations within the church, and gives a list of two periodicals put out by the church (both of which I have included in this bibliography).

____. 1972 Edition, p. 38. Same as the 1962 Edition but excludes the organizations within the church and does not list the periodicals.

____. 1973 Edition, p. 39.

____. 1976 Edition, p. 43. Same as the 1973 Edition but excludes two of the officers.

____. 1978 Edition, p. 42. This is the last edition that the church is mentioned in. The last edition I looked at was from 1987.

Lawrence City Directory. (Sioux Center, Iowa:R.C. Polk Co., 1907), p. 16. This is the first time the church is listed even though it was founded in Lawrence in 1896. The address was 13 E. Henry — organized 1898 — membership was 36: Pastor, Frank J. Smith.

____. 1908–1909 Edition, p. 18.

____. 1911 Edition, p. 18. Same address but listing only 30 members and Pastor J.M. Venarable.

____. 1913–1914 Edition, p.16. Now located on 1239 NJ with a Pastor John Lutz.

____. 1915 Edition, p. 16. Membership is 35.

____. 1917 Edition, p. 14.

____. 1919 Edition, p. 13. Membership is 28, with an Elder Martin Fears.

Lincoln, C. Eric. *The Black Experience in Religion.* (New York: Doubleday, 1974), p. 265. Tells of an article written by Arthur Dobrin (which I cited in this bibliography).

Logan, Rayford W. *The Negro in American Life and Thought.* (New York: The Dial Press, 1954). Gives an account as to what life was like for Negroes from 1877–1901.

Marty, Martin E. *The New Shape of American Religion.* (New York: Harper & Brothers, 1958), p. 164. This author does not like the fact that there are so many Churches of God with different endings, etc.

Mathison, Richard R. *Faiths, Cults and Sects of America.* (New York: Bobbs-Merrill Co., 1960), pp. 245–247. This is the source that Dobrin used when he mistakingly thought that F.S. Cherry was the founder of the church. Mathison gives no bibliography or citation as to where he gathered his inaccurate information.

Mayer, F.E. *The Religious Bodies of America.* (St. Louis: Concordia Publishing House, 1958), p. 523. Lists the name of the church and the doctrine. It is similar to the summary found in the *Encyclopedia of American Religion.*

Mead, Frank S. *Handbook of Denominations in the U.S.* (New York: Pierce & Smith, 1951), p. 57. Tells of the number of members and churches for 1951 and gives a description of the organizational structure.

____. *Handbook of Denominations in the U.S.* Second Revised Edition. (New York: Abingdon Press, 1961), p. 76. Tells of the number of churches and members for 1961 and gives a description of the organizational structure.

____. *The American Mercury.* "The Lunatic Fringe of Religion." Vol. 52, No. 206, Feb. 1941, pp. 172–173. Talks about the church as being before the Father Divine era and that Crowdy was referred to as the Great Father Abraham.

Melton, Gordon J. *A Directory of Religious Bodies.* (New York: Garland Publishing, 1977), pp. 109 & 273. Mentions the COGSOC under Black Jews and gives the name of H.Z. Plummer who was head of the church until his death in 1980.

____. *Encyclopedia of American Religion.* Detroit: Gale Research Co., 1987, p.674. Tells of the doctrine, number of churches and membership, and educational facilities. Unfortunately this information gives the reader an inaccurate source which is Arthur Huff Fauset's *Black Gods of the Metropolis.* (Philadelphia: University of Pennsylvania Press, 1944.) Fauset talks at great length of The Church of God but does not mention The Church of God and Saints of Christ.

____. *The Encyclopedia of American Religion.* (North Carolina: McGrath Publishing Co., 1978), Vol. 2 , pp.330–332, 522–523. Refers to the church as "Black Jews" and gives a summary from the Census of Religious Bodies 1936.

Murphy, T.F. *Census of Religious Bodies* 1926. (Washington D.C.: U.S. Government Printing Office, 1928).

Murphy, T.F. *Census of Religious Bodies: 1936 — Vol. 2 — Part 1.* (Washington D.C.: U.S. Government Printing Office, 1941), pp. 433–440. Tells of the history, doctrine, organization, and work of the church. Its main emphasis is statistics on the 213 U.S. churches of 1936.

Murray, Florence. *The Negro Handbook.* (New York: Wendell Malliet and Company, 1942), p. 97. Gives some statistics from *Census of Religious Bodies,1936.*

____. *The Negro Handbook.* (New York: Current Reference Publications, 1944), pp. 29, 79. States that the church is a black Jewish church. The value is $544,270 with 37,084 members. Page. 29 gives statistics which state an increase in negro attendance of 24.7% from 1906 to 1916, 13.1% from 1916 to 1926, and 8.8% from 1926 to 1936.

____. *The Negro Handbook.* (New York: Macmillan Co., 1949), p. 288. Gives Plummer's 1949 address.

Neill, Stephen. *Christian Missions.* (Baltimore: Penguin, 1966).

Nelsen, Yokley, Nelsen. *The Black Church in America.* (New York: Basic Books Inc., 1971). Tells of the fact that even in a book of this title the Church of God and Saints of Christ fails to be included. This is my observation.

O'Brien, T.C. *Corpus Dictionary of Western Churches.* (Washington: Cleavland Press, 1970), p. 192. Tells of the services' being Pentecostal (refers to the Grove faction) in nature and gives some statistics.

Official State Atlas of Kansas. (Philadelphia: L.H. Everts and Company, 1887), pp. 1–2, 24–25.

Pennington, Dorothy L. *The Histories and Cultural Roles of Black Churches in Lawrence, Kansas.* (Unpublished, 1983), p. 2. The church is mentioned; its location is given as south Lawrence.

Philadelphia Press, January 13, 1902, page 3 column 7. "Bishop Is Accused of Anarchy." Documents the historical fact that black ministers of the day felt threatened by Crowdy's charisma and preaching style. This article also exemplifies the fact that Crowdy was not always recieved well, this time he had the backing of the Mayor (Ashbridge of Philadelphia).

Philadelphia Sunday Press, July 13, 1902. "I am de only Prophet foh dis generation." An article which depicts the reporters' bigotry of the time and gives pictures of Crowdy and the COGSOC grocery store.

Philadelphia Tribune, June 28, 1913. "Church of God — Bishops in Court." The battle for head bishop between J.S. Dickerson and J.M. Grove.

Religious Bodies 1916. (Washington D.C.: Dept. of Commerce, Bureau of the Census Gov't Printing Office, 1919).

Rolner, Murray. "Black and Being Jewish," *The National Jewish Monthly*, October 1972, pp. 38–43. Erroneously calls Crowdy "Crowley."

Schick, Kaethe and Hoggard, Kathy. "The Black Community in Lawrence, 1870–1915." Contains helpful information about Lawrence.

Salisbury, W. Seward. *Religion in American Culture.* (Chicago: Dorsey Press, 1964), p.157, 445. Tells of the category of storefront churches of which the Church of God and Saints of Christ is included.

Schoeps, Hans-Joachim. *The Religions of Mankind.* (Garden City, New York: Doubleday, 1968).

Sernett, Milton C. *Afro-American Religious History-A Documentary Witness.* (Durham: Duke University Press, 1985), pp. 390, 391, 395, 397. Tells of a Miles Mark Fischer who wrote the chapter on "Organized Religion and the Cults."

Special Reports-Religious Bodies 1906. (Washington D.C.: Dept. of Commerce and Labor, Bureau of the Census Gov't Printing Office, 1910).

Sperry, Willard. *Religion in America.* (New York: MacMillan Co., 1946), pp. 72, 288. A brief mention of the church's existence is given.

Stone, Sara Margaret. "Transmission and Performance practice in an urban black denomination — The Church of God and Saints of Christ." (Kent State Univ., Ph.D., 1985), 442 pp. Provides a discussion of factions, of which she cites three.

Sundkler, Bengt. *Bantu Prophets in South Africa.* (London: Int'l African Institute for Oxford Press, 1961), pp. 72–3. Talks about Enoch Mgijima who was an elder in the COGSOC in Africa.

The Virginian-Pilot, April 1, 1988. "Black Jews step out of the shadows." Describes the land that the church owns.

Tinney, James S. "Black Jews: A House Divided." *Christianity Today,* Dec. 7, 1973, pp.52–54. This source gives some interesting data on the rules within a temple service. Tells of two distinctive practices of using water for communion and smearing exteriors of homes with animal blood during passover.

Trepp, Leo. *Judaism: Development and Life.* (Belmont: Wadsworth, 1982).

Walls, Bishop W. *The African American Methodist Episcopal Church: Reality of Black Church.* (Charlotte: A.M.E. Zion publishing house., 1974), p. 490. Contains a brief mention of the church.

Washington, Joseph R. *Black Sects and Cults.* (New York: Doubleday, 1972), pp. 132–133. This author talked with a member of the church, Bishop Howard Z. Plummer.

Watson, E.O. *Yearbook of the Churches 1921–1922.* (Washington D.C.: Hayworth Publishing Co., 1922), p. 56. Tells of the history, doctrine, and polity of the church.

Weisbord, Robert S. "Black Hebrew Israelites". *Judaism,* Winter 1975, Issue No. 93, Vol. 24, No. 1, pp. 23–38. He refers to the influence of Prophet Crowdy, who "revealed to his worshipful disciples that the Lost Tribes of Israel were the forebears of American Negroes," and thus Crowdy might have been the "intellectual father" of the "Hebrew Israelites in Dimona."

Wilder, Daniel B. *Annals of Kansas*. (Topeka: G.W. Martin, 1875), p. 404. There is one line referring to the church: "The Church of God and Saints of Christ met at Lawrence." [April 15, 1904].

Wilmore, Gayrand S. *Black Religion and Black Radicalism*. (New York:Doubleday, 1972), p. 179. Tells of the African bishop that was trained by Crowdy and was sent back to Africa to establish a church there. The bishop was John Msikinya.

Williams, John and Ploski, Harry A. *Negro Almanac: A reference work on the Afro-American*. 4th edition. (New York: John Wiley and Sons, 1983), p. 1272. Briefly mentions the church.

Williams, Ora. *Directories of Churches and Religious Organizations in Iowa*. (Des Moines: The Historical RecordSurvey, 1940), p. 71. Mentions the church on 928 W. 12th St. in Des Moines with an Evangelist E. Williams of 2413 Garfield Ave.

Windsor, Rudolph and Steven, Jacobs. *The Hebrew Heritage of our West African Ancestors*. (Wilmington Delaware: Roselee, June 1971).

Zavelo, Donald B. *The Black Entrepreneur in Lawrence,Kansas, 1900–1915*. (KU honors thesis, 1975), p.12. Briefly mentions the church.

DATE DUE